backyard blueprints

backyard blueprints

David Stevens

photography by Jerry Harpur

STERLING
INNOVATION
A Division of Sterling Publishing Co., Inc.
New York

Editor **Judy Spours**
Designer **Maggie Town**
Illustrator **Lizzie Sanders**

**Library of Congress
Cataloging-in-Publication Data Available**

10   9   8   7   6   5   4   3

Published in 2002 by Sterling Publishing Co., Inc.
387 Park Avenue South, New York, NY 10016

First published in Great Britain in 2002
by Jacqui Small
an imprint of Aurum Press Ltd.
25 Bedford Avenue, London, WC1B 3AT

Text © David Stevens 2002
Photography © Jerry Harpur 2002
Illustrations, layout and design © Jacqui Small 2002

Distributed in Canada by Sterling Publishing
c/o Canadian Manda Group, 165 Dufferin Street,
Toronto, Ontario, Canada M6K 3H6

Printed and bound in China
All rights reserved

ISBN 13: 978-1-4027-3726-8
ISBN 10: 1-4027-3726-2

contents

Blueprints in preparation   7

Blueprints for design   17

    Style uncovered   20

    Controlling space   33

    Designing with space   45

    Material world   56

Blueprints for furnishing   65

    Outdoor furniture   69

    Water features   76

    Work and play   85

    Arbours, arches and pergolas   92

    Ornament   100

    Designing with light   106

Blueprints for planting   113

    Designing with plants   116

    Shape, texture and colour   122

    Particular places   132

Index   142

Acknowledgements   144

blueprints
in preparation

above Patios are all about shelter, seclusion, and a wonderful feeling of intimacy – they are where small is beautiful. Here is the perfect outdoor room, wrapped with planting that demands minimal maintenance, yet provides interest throughout the year.

right It is incredible how such a small space can feel so large; the secret is disguising the boundaries completely. Pink lilies in the foreground lead the eye to a cool and inviting arbor that forms an oasis in the heart of a city.

backyards have great potential to become perfect outdoor rooms, yet they are often the most undervalued of garden spaces. They can be neat, colorful, practical, easy to maintain, and, above all else, fun. A backyard can be a multifunctional space in which plants take their place alongside areas in which to sit, dine, and entertain. Children can play here, herbs and salads have room to grow, and everyday tasks can be enjoyed in the open air. Here is a place that will accommodate an area for workouts or a quiet corner for study; and woven around and within the yard can be all kinds of ornament and focal points, from built-in barbecues to raised plant beds, water features to eye-catching statuary.

Just how you can achieve any or all of this is my job to tell, as I have been creating yards of every shape and size for the past thirty years or so. There are, of course, design principles, tricks of the trade, and good common-sense rules that I am happy to share. The key point is to figure out what kind of person you are and what you and the family really want from your backyard. Inspiration will be all about you, so do not get seduced by fashion or the latest television craze for a particular style or makeover. Backyards are driven by your personality, and the best design will fit you like a glove. It will not be some fancy and impractical vignette from a glossy magazine, rather a slightly haphazard, comfortable, and eclectic composition. It may be vibrant or cool, chic or crisply architectural, but it will certainly represent you and your ideas and needs.

Nobody wants a garden design, but everyone wants a finished garden; the design is simply a vehicle that takes you from conception to completion. The style or mood you incorporate and the features you choose come later, but the first job is to get a feel of what surrounds you. The constraints, characteristics, and advantages of the plot will define the design process, setting physical parameters. The temptation is to rush out and get started right away, but you should not crystallize your ideas too soon. Take your time, settle into your home and yard, however unpromising the latter may be, and just start to get a feel of the place.

preparing for action

There are a thousand books that go into the detail of measuring a garden and I am not going to do so here, except to make a few points about accuracy. The reason we take measurements is so that we can draw the garden to scale, which allows the quantities of plants and materials to be accurately assessed. You would never think of buying a pair of shoes or suit of clothes on guesswork, and a garden is no different — accuracy is everything. A scale drawing simply represents the yard at a smaller size. For example, a scale of 1 to 100 will produce a drawing in which the yard is one hundred times smaller than the actual plot, but in exact proportion to it.

Another reason for preparing a scale drawing is that very often, particularly with an awkwardly shaped yard, the true shape looks quite different on paper from what you perceive. For example, I recently undertook a commission for a design of a long and narrow town lot. Once it was drawn out, the clients could not believe just how long it was, although this was a real asset, allowing me to create a number of quite separate garden rooms. This was an approach they would never have taken without seeing the proportions drawn out on paper. The scale drawing is simply your garden in miniature, allowing you to plan on a table top, saving you time, effort, and often a good deal of hard-earned cash.

It is sensible, if not vital, to allocate a realistic budget for your yard right from the start. Most people underestimate garden expenditure, but if you consider it as an outside room, then building and furnishing a garden is not much different from work inside the home. It will inevitably be the hard landscape of paving, walling, steps, and other major features that will take the lion's share of any budget, and these costs broadly equate to conventional building work. Plants and planting are relatively inexpensive, particularly in a yard where space is at a premium. It is worth stressing that you should not offer hard landscape work to builders, however keen and persuasive they may be. Builders are usually great at working vertically but relatively unskilled at moving horizontally to lay paving. The scale drawing of the yard can form the basis for good landscapers to quote in competition.

left Eclecticism lies at the heart of much good exterior design, and this delightful garden takes part of its inspiration from the vibrancy of Moroccan culture. Brightly colored walls, tiles, pots, and planting mingle to create an exciting yet deliciously personal space.

above right There is a narrow line between complexity and overcomplication, and walking it is entirely dependent on the creator of a garden. This is a remarkable patio with a finely worked floor and focal points by the bucketful! Many would say it is just too busy, but I think it is fantastic.

Find them by recommendation or through a reputable trade organization, and always have a good look at their work before you award the contract.

There is nothing difficult in designing a garden or yard; most professional designers adhere to a tried and tested set of rules that they know will work under most circumstances. The difference between you and a professional is that you have time on your side; you can quietly assess and absorb all that is around you, taking in the ambience and characteristics of the place. This is a huge advantage, which should allow you to create something that is quietly measured rather than hastily scrambled. The best outside rooms take their surrounds into account, embracing good views, making the most of forgotten corners, and cleverly concealing the utilitarian or ugly. A year is perfect to get to know a garden location; with the turning of the seasons you will see the sun pitch higher and lower, track a prevailing wind, and see which plants appear when. You will start to appreciate the advantages and limitations of the yard, which will in turn suggest the basis of a design.

Perhaps the most important factor, so often overlooked, is the relationship between inside and outside space, the way in which the yard sits with the house it adjoins. Does it flow smoothly out from French or sliding doors; is it set deep in a basement well with narrow steps for access; or is it tucked at the side of the house, leading out to a more expansive space at the rear? Its situation will have a real impact on how we reach the yard and will almost certainly determine the treatment of the immediate area in terms of materials, colors, and plants. As soon as you move from inside to out, the impact of views, good or bad, becomes apparent. A fine building in the distance, a glimpse of a spire, or a beautiful tree or group of shrubs in a neighbor's yard can be emphasized or framed. This is "borrowed landscape" that allows you to maximize your own space by using someone else's. But on the debit side, high oppressive walls of adjoining properties, perhaps with windows that overlook, are often a real headache in town. Views of the back of someone's garage or the top of a shed looming over a fence are unattractive, while the wrong species of tree, grown to maturity with heavy foliage, can block light and drains and sap all the available goodness from the soil. With some thought and a little ingenuity, though, a problem can always be solved or screened.

the character of the plot

The course of the sun throughout the day is vitally important, impacting on where you sit, eat, and carry on much of your outdoor living. One great advantage of a sheltered yard where wind chill is reduced is that it can often be used in winter, but remember that the sun swings lower in the sky and shadows cast from walls and buildings will be correspondingly longer. It can be useful just to draw an arc of the sun's path at the top of your survey drawing to track its position throughout the day.

The height, position, and materials of walls have an impact on the yard design. Walls in poor condition may well need remedial attention and, if they adjoin living areas within the house, can be painted to pick up and extend an interior color scheme. Or they may become vehicles for murals, containers, water features, trellis, or planting. The same assessment applies to fences and even hedges, which can be clipped, shaped, and trained. If a backyard slopes, it is important to check out exactly where and how much it does so. Slopes determine the position of steps, ramps, and split-level features. If the yard is already terraced, you can measure each drop with a tape and add them together, giving the overall fall. It is also relatively easy, particularly in a small area, to judge the drop of a slope by eye, lining it up and measuring from eye level to ground.

Inside the house, we pay a good deal of attention to the floor, and so we should outside, noting its materials and condition. It could be of well-laid brick or tile paving, poorly set precast concrete slabs, broken concrete, or just plain soil. If the surface is sound and acceptable, it could fit perfectly with any proposed design, needing minimal or no disturbance at all. If the materials, say of brick or tile, are in good condition but poorly laid or in the wrong place, it may well be possible to lift and store them, saving a good deal of expense later on. If a surface is solid but ugly, it may be possible to pave or deck over it, using it as a foundation. There does need to be enough depth that the additional thickness of the new material

NOTES:
Brick house

Garden sheltered –
no prevailing wind

Soil quality – heavy

6-ft-high panel fence   gate   garage – brick – tile roof

3.1   30 ft from house

2.0

3.0   5.0

Rowan tree in corner

soil sample ph 7.0

overlooked from
neighbor's window

canopy extends
8 ft from rear fence

6-ft-high panel
fence

GARDEN FLAT AND
ALL LAID TO LAWN

6-ft-high panel
fence

soil sample ph 6.9

1.1

18-in square paving –
flagstones

manhole cover

1.2

start running
measurements

window   door

2 ft   2.6   3.5   4.5   5.0

NORTH

surveying the site

The survey is the first step of the design
process. First, I take "running measurements",
with the tape laid out right across and
down the garden. All appropriate details and
features are marked, including the building
itself, position of doors and windows, drains,
and changes of level.

Check soil type, the boundary materials, and
existing planting. Note good or bad views,
the direction of a prevailing wind, and the
orientation of the yard.

In doing this, you will almost certainly start
to get a real feeling of the plot – the sunny
and shady areas, how you move around the
space, the potential for a particular feature,
or a focal point. This will shape your thinking
about how to develop the garden.

does not bridge a dampproofing built into the house walls, which is normally set about 6 inches below door sills. Also note the position of drains or manholes, and never plan to pave or lay a surface over them.

Part of the yard may simply be soil, and many urban gardens, particularly those adjoining older properties, have been overworked with little addition of organic material. As a result, the soil will almost certainly be impoverished, and it is a good idea to check its acidity or alkalinity with a simple soil-testing kit, which may dictate what you can grow. It is also worth noting what grows well elsewhere in the neighborhood. If there are already plants, shrubs, or trees in the yard, try to identify them and plot their positions. Quite unexpected treasures may make an appearance at different times of the year. Just occasionally, the urge to remove existing trees or planting to start with a clean slate seems overpowering. It is wiser to wait, as an apparently unpromising shrub, or a tree thinned to allow more light and air into a particular area, might form the basis of a planting scheme. A tree might play host to a built-in seat, rising majestically through a deck or simply casting dappled shade as shelter from a hot sun.

At the earliest stage, the provision of services, primarily water for irrigation and electricity for power, is worth thinking about. Yards can often be extremely dry, as high walls and overhanging roofs create rain shadows. Irrigation can be as simple as a well-positioned faucet or as sophisticated as a fully automated and computerized system. Electricity will power lighting, pool and water feature equipment, and also operate greenhouse propagators and ventilation. Both can work on a main system in which the service can be picked up at any point in the yard. If the facilities are installed before any new paving or other structural work takes place, disruption will obviously be kept to a minimum. Needless to say, these are specialized jobs, and if you are in any doubt whatsoever, seek help from a professional.

The point of all this initial fact-finding is to get a feel of what you have already got in your backyard and how it can evolve to become an integral part of your life. Having all the aspects and implications of the plot at your fingertips will give you the tools to achieve a unique and personal backyard. Armed with this information, fueled with enthusiasm, and inspired by a wealth of ideas, it is now time to get started!

left The use here of bold color, simple yet subtle geometric shapes, and architectural planting are a perfect foil to the house on the one hand and harsh semidesert on the other. This is the perfect example of environmentally sensitive gardening, respecting rather than turning its back on its surroundings.

blueprints for design

above Patios and yards are multifunctional places, and the smaller they are, the better the planning needs to be. Sitting and eating outside are among life's pleasures, particularly if the areas are sheltered by walls and bathed in sunlight filtering through foliage above.

right A formal design is visually reassuring – everything is in its place, neatly controlled, and with an air of permanence. Perspective is strong here, with the eye being led from interior sheltered space, over the lawn and pool, to focus on the tumbling cascade at the end of the yard.

good design is invariably simple – complicated ideas spell disaster in many a yard. In fact, the smaller the yard or patio area, the simpler the design should be. It is important not to mistake simplicity for subtlety, though, which is a welcome ingredient that can add immeasurably to any composition.

Until relatively recently, fashion did not greatly influence exterior design, but there is no doubt that certain styles have now become trends. This tendency has been driven by the media and by a huge growth in garden shows and garden centers. Yet fashion is the enemy of good design, bringing immediacy rather than a longer-term involvement with a developing environment. Inspiration is something different, and can come from virtually anywhere, including a judicious viewing of garden and television shows. Using inspiration to create something that is just right for you is quite different from simply copying an idea designed to suit a completely different set of circumstances. The reason why yards are different from one another is to do with the personalities of their owners. You could have a hundred identical plots of the same shape, slope, and aspect, but all would turn out quite differently, depending on the needs of those that tended them.

A yard is almost certainly the largest space over which you will have complete control, as virtually everything else in this life – including our clothes and often our houses – is designed for us. Our freedom in our yards is an enormously exciting proposition, providing us with our own spaces to do with what we will. Even if we employ help with the conception, the mark of good designers is that they are simply facilitators, not dictators who impose their ideas on others. As a designer, it is my job to gather needs, ideas, and ideals, and mold them, along with my own experience and inspiration, into a workable composition. If you are designing your own yard, the very same process applies for you.

Good or great yards have an almost indefinable feeling of "rightness," both with the properties they adjoin and the people they serve. Such places are never pretentious and are almost invariably comfortable, and the best of them, whether ancient or modern in design, are full of vibrancy and charm.

style uncovered

Style is an overplayed commodity in today's gardening circles. Many of the best compositions never set out to be Italianate, cottage, Japanese, or anything else specific; rather, they simply happen around their creators. Instead of style, perhaps we should read lifestyle, something that reflects the way we live and those who will use the yard. This is where that wonderful quality of eclecticism comes in, bringing with it a diversity of influences, but rolling them together into something that is perfect to the owner.

Designing any yard is largely to do with the manipulation of space and, even more specifically, with pattern-making. Patterns can be formal and balanced, asymmetrical, freeform, or even deconstructivist. The real point is not to get hung up on such names; neither you nor a designer should set out purposefully to design, say, a "deconstructivist" garden. The whole planning sequence works the other way around. You start with a hit list of needs, likes, family pets, and the proportions and situation of the yard itself. All of these will suggest the style you end up with. In other words, self-analysis is required first and action second.

If we assume that personality drives our lifestyle, it follows that it will have influenced the house we choose to live in and the artefacts we gather around us. We may be traditional in our outlook, with a liking for period furniture and paintings, or rather more contemporary, with an affinity for clean geometry or simple fluid shapes. Right at the far end of the scale, we might be completely avant-garde, with a radical style that embraces art and architecture at the outer limits of design. It is worth underlining the point that no particular style is any better or worse than another, they are simply different – although it is certainly true that formalism was born far longer ago than deconstructivism. Remember, too, that you might have a formal, asymmetric, or freeform Japanese, English, or Mediterranean yard – culture or geography have nothing to do with the basic design styles.

It is also worth remembering that a yard need not be a static affair. After all, we often change rooms inside the home by moving furniture and screens or re-thinking color schemes. This same philosophy is rarely employed outside, which is a pity, because although you may not be able to alter a basic style, you can certainly bring considerable influence to bear on the incidental features. Moving focal points or ornaments can lead your eye in a completely different direction; seats can be re-positioned to embrace a new view, and a new planting scheme, like wallpaper inside the house, may have dramatic visual implications.

right This yard is tiny, a delightful microcosm set in the heart of London. The style is unashamedly Japanese, interpreted by a sensitive eye with great skill. The meandering stream and paths increase a feeling of space, while the simple use of ground cover provides great continuity.

left Framing a view can achieve many things; here it not only focuses attention on the yard below, but also screens a row of houses beyond. The sitting area is contained within its own "room" by the wing of planting, which in turn encourages you to find out what lies beyond.

formal

Formal designs are balanced affairs in which one part of a yard mirrors another. They sit comfortably with a regularly modeled house façade and can be particularly attractive within the intimate confines of a courtyard, where a simple axis or vista can be flanked by paved areas, trellising, grass, or planting. Such compositions often benefit from carefully positioned focal points, which might be statuary, a water feature, seat, or, if space allows, a small summerhouse or garden building. Planting can either be similarly balanced or placed asymmetrically within a formal composition. The latter means that groups of plants or colors can visually offset one another in different parts of the yard.

Formal designs are relatively static affairs, controlled compositions that offer measured movement and activity rather than encouraging boisterous games. Such gardens tend, therefore, to be set pieces rather than family affairs, although in the right situation there is little wrong with that. People often only think of formality in traditional or classical terms, while in fact this same style can be equally effective in a strikingly modern setting.

Formality is a measured design style that can be ideal in the confines of a small town garden. The centerpiece of this yard is a simple rectangular pool, shown in the photograph on the left, with a seat to one side and an arch to the other, both set on a cross axis. The main view from the house is first held by the centrally placed fountain (pictured far left) and then moves on up the steps and through the arch toward the more distant parts of the composition (pictured above).

1 Bridge to far garden **2** Hedge
3 Rose arch **4** Planting **5** Containers **6** Light fixtures **7** Climbing plants **8** Step **9** Light fixtures **10** Arum lilies **11** Clipped yews
12 Mature tree **13** Mirror **14** Arch
15 Bubble fountain **16** Seat **17** Pool
18 Chair **19** Inset tiles **20** Steps
21 Clipped box cubes **22** Flagstone paving

While the modern movement revolutionized architecture, it took rather longer for this wonderfully adaptable style to find its way into the yard. Geometry is paramount in an asymmetrical design, but relies for its success on achieving balance with shapes and volumes of variable size. This yard demonstrates that rectangles can be subtly overlapped to form areas of paving, planting, and water that combine to produce an elegant and practical space. Contrasting materials, including floating stainless-steel balls, set up a wonderful dialogue with the black concrete columns, metal decking strips, and impeccably detailed plant boxes that lead your eye across the pool.

1 Stone chips **2** Planting
3 Boundary wall **4** Steps
5 Specimen silver birch
6 Raised beds **7** Upper deck
8 Hydraulic table **9** Step
10 Stainless steel balls
11 Pool **12** Steel and wooden decking
13 Alpine plants in chips
14 "Thyme" stepping stones
15 Black concrete columns
16 Low wall

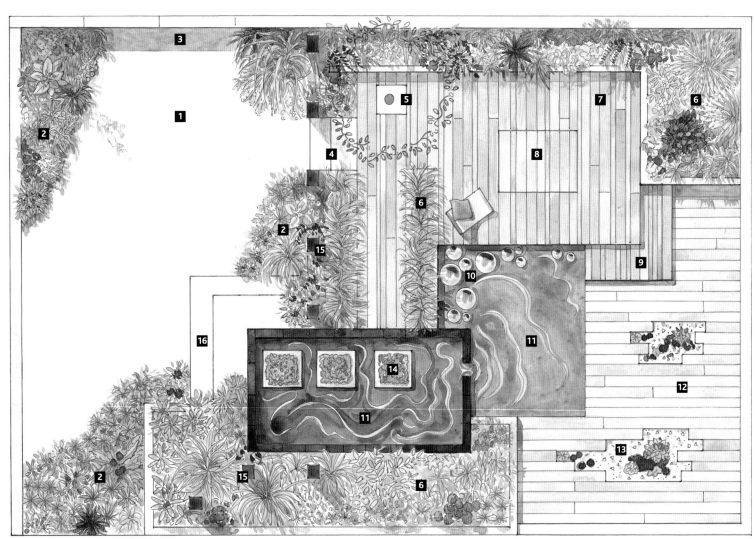

asymmetrical

Asymmetrical yards or areas also achieve balance, but in a quite different way. Asymmetry was born out of the modern movement, which broke down the traditional and classical style of design that had dominated architecture and the organization of exterior space for several thousand years. In this case, balance is brought about not by regularly positioned pieces or features, but by one part of the composition offsetting another in a different part of the yard. The easiest analogy is that of two weights positioned around a fulcrum. Formality demands that the weights are the same, placed equidistantly on each side of the fulcrum. Asymmetry, on the other hand, can use dissimilar weights, but will still achieve balance if the heavier is closer and the lighter farther away from the fulcrum.

This way, a paved area on one side and adjoining the rear of a house could be balanced by the vertical emphasis of a tree set diagonally across the garden toward the bottom. Alternatively, a small water feature could be offset by a raised bed in another location. Asymmetry is a dynamic design form, associating well with many building styles, particularly those of a more modern nature.

freeform

Freeform patterns are surprisingly useful in a small space, where their fluid lines can detract from oppressive rectangular boundaries. A freeform yard at its simplest could be just a circle, inside which might be a paved, graveled or decked area, with planting around. The introduction of plants will soften the perimeter walls or fences and, if these are completely screened, provide the illusion of the yard being larger than it actually is. In a larger space, the shapes can either overlap one another or flow in a continuous pattern around the yard.

The secret of freeform is to be both generous and simple with the outline; busy or convoluted shapes are hard on the eye. It is also important to be conscious of how the internal freeform pattern, often called positive space, relates to the surrounding boundaries. There should always be a comfortable balance, with no "pinch-points" or excessively narrow borders that make it difficult to provide planting. The area between the freeform positive pattern and the boundaries is referred to as negative space; the two should be in harmony.

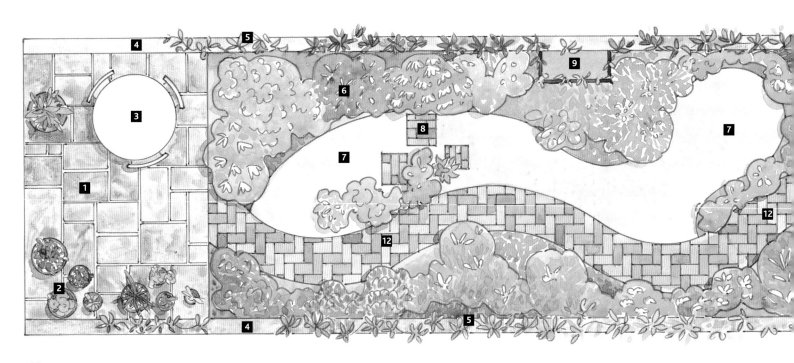

A freeform design appears to be the antithesis of control, but in fact a feeling of space and proportion is vital if such a yard is to succeed. In this tiny but beautiful yard, paving, paths, and planting are woven into a delicious journey from the house to a secret arbor set with flowers and foliage.

It all looks so simple, but it takes a huge amount of skill and experience to create a garden of such worth.

1 Flagstone paved terrace **2** Containers
3 Table and chairs **4** Boundary wall
5 Climbing plants **6** Mixed planting
7 Lawn **8** Brick panels **9** Arbor
10 Fernery **11** Archway **12** Brick path

We are not all lucky enough to have a view of the Golden Gate Bridge, but it does underline the point that "borrowed" landscape can be a very real bonus. The shapes of this terrace echo the line of the distant hills, but the color and capricious outline are more reminiscent of the Surrealist artist Jean Miró. This is a joyful, free-thinking design, but it is highly personal, not to everyone's taste.

1 Sun loungers 2 Planting in containers
3 Stationary benches 4 Terrace walls and
rails 5 Table and chairs 6 Overlaid pattern
of spots 7 Freestanding chair 8 Screening
panels 9/10 Large uplighter fixtures
11 Metal overhead rails

deconstructivist

At the opposite end of the design spectrum from formality is deconstructivism. If we assume that garden design is an art form, which it most certainly is, then the boundaries of that art form should constantly be expanded to take in new ideas. Deconstructivism is really a form that takes apart many of the perceived rules of exterior design and re-assembles them in an abstract pattern. As is the case with modern painting, this is not a random process and you need to have considerable design experience to produce a successful composition. This said, a good deconstructivist yard, using leading-edge materials such as glass, steel, and plastics, can produce stunning results that correspond perfectly to modern architecture.

One of the real problems with garden design is the fact that it has become a largely retrospective art form, looking back rather than forward for its inspiration. While history and past styles can often provide a basis, we should not necessarily be bound by them. There are, of course, many fine traditional gardens, but it is always stimulating to explore new materials, new patterns, and new ideas to create original spaces.

compiling a moodboard

You will naturally gain inspiration for your design from all kinds of places, including books, magazines, and photographs taken of other yards you particularly like. Instead of filing them away in a folder, pin them up on a "mood-board" where you can see them from day to day; the kitchen is often the best place. Such images might include well-planted beds or color schemes; details of paths, paving, or walling; or perhaps a clever water feature. You could add a swatch of subtle wood stains for a possible deck, or a small sample bag of gravel. Over a period of time, you may tire of a certain style, so take that particular image down and replace it with new ideas as they come along. See how everything stands the test of time for a month or so, and invite everybody in the household to add their own moods to the board. All of this will help you to focus on the kind of design you feel most comfortable with, and it is a genuinely helpful way of getting to know what you want.

right This moodboard is the starting point for the design of the garden featured on page 68. It includes photographs of planting ideas and features in other yards, materials that might eventually be chosen as hard landscaping, and drawings of ornamental pieces. A rough sketch of the yard is added to the board, and the whole scheme begins to take shape.

controlling space

The manipulation of space provides interest in many a yard, which can itself be compared to the rooms inside the house. Open-plan homes become a good deal more attractive when you move from room to room or area to area. What the divisions are made from is largely unimportant in spatial terms; the appeal is in the act of discovery and invitation. A garden is really no different, and the average yard is possibly no bigger than the house it adjoins. The real point of the analogy is the creation of interest; if you enter a yard where everything is visible at a glance, the end result is pretty boring. If, on the other hand, you view your yard, however small it may be, and are confronted by a series of individual sections or screens, there is a whole new experience in store in the generation of the classic ingredients of tension, mystery, and surprise.

Before we start looking in detail at the space of the yard, it is worth thinking for a moment about what may happen outside its boundaries. Here there can be good, bad, or indifferent views, with real implications for how you view the space. I cannot stress strongly enough that house, yard, and any views beyond are quite inseparable; the "borrowed landscape" outside the yard is inevitably a part of it. Not all of us are lucky enough to have a wonderful view, but if you do, then for goodness sake do not throw it away. Frame it with planting or carefully positioned small trees to bring everything into focus. This

left While rooms inside the home are relatively static affairs, those outside can be clothed with the patterns of ever-changing foliage. Boundaries can be softened, and the subtle placement of focal points can draw us into a world far divorced from everyday life.

right There is a wonderful contrast here between the clean lines of furniture and decking and the luxuriant planting, which presses in on the space with overtones of a jungle clearing.

left That element of what lies beyond is always important, and if you can draw the eye toward a distant sky or wider landscape, the yard will naturally feel larger and more interesting.

principle of visual control is important, since a wide-open view is often far less dramatic than one that is subtly contained. It is like a painting that is fine on the canvas but altogether sharper when surrounded by a sympathetic frame.

On a slightly more mundane, but nevertheless just as important, level is what I call "merging." In most small areas it is the boundaries that are dominant; while these are sometimes high walls, more often than not they are lower, perhaps 5 feet or less. In this case they will almost certainly adjoin someone else's yard, where in turn planting may be visible. Sometimes foliage may overhang and, rather than zealously cutting it back, it is better to make the most of it. Why not match the species, and if possible extend the group so that the

visual interest

The vital garden ingredients of tension, mystery, and surprise can work in both formal and informal settings to lead us through the composition on a journey of discovery. In a flowing freeform design, on the left, a path mysteriously disappears from view. This is a simple yet effective device that adds immeasurably to any yard. In a more formal setting, on the right, hedging and planting form a doorway into the next outdoor room. A partial view is always intriguing; as you approach, there is a buildup of tension and expectancy; through the gap, tension is released and replaced by the surprise of a new vista.

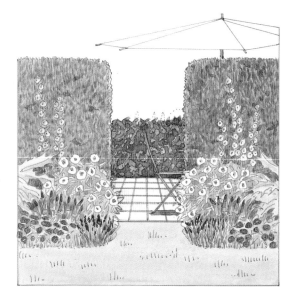

boundary is hidden and the two outdoor spaces run seamlessly together? The smaller a yard, the more advantageous it is to decide to screen or at least soften the boundaries, and if you can meld two adjoining yards together so that you are not quite sure where one finishes and the next begins, then the spaces will both tend to feel larger.

Of course it is also quite possible to have a simply awful view, one that is difficult to screen in its entirety. Very often the act of trying to block it out simply draws attention to it, rather like placing a pot or statue on a drain inspection cover, so it may well be better to create interest elsewhere in the composition. If you positively direct the line of sight to a focal point situated in another part of the yard, this becomes the major attraction above all else.

Focal points, whatever they are, have the ability to draw the eye and create visual movement, which in turn will be a major driving force in how we perceive the yard. It follows that many focal points, such as seats, gazebos, arbors, and even statues or pools, attract us toward them. This is all well and good, but once we reach the focal point, we will then have to turn back to return, and the reverse view must be just as good. There is little point in being taken somewhere wonderful only then to see the side of someone's garage or perhaps your oil storage tank in your line of sight on your return journey through the yard.

above It is all here – the carefully placed pots of Arum lilies that focus the view, a rose-smothered arch that beckons you forward, and a tantalizing glimpse of what lies ahead.

left A room with a view, but what a delicious transition between inside and out! You are drawn from house to balcony before the eye drifts out to the roofscape beyond. The secret is foreground interest, a "pause point'"and the place for afternoon tea or a sundowner.

right This is the reverse view of the picture on the left and proves the point that both vistas are vitally important. This really is a delightful yard, too small for lawn, but a haven of containers and potted plants that lead out from the house.

linking inside and out

A backyard is often small, but rather than seeing this as a drawback we should embrace both its practicality in terms of maintenance and its potential for all kinds of visual effects. This is where the importance of linking internal and external space becomes important. If we can think of the yard as an outside room that extends our living space, then it is much easier to make the areas compatible.

Unsuccessful yards so often turn their back on the house they adjoin, which is a psychological barrier from using them, particularly during the winter months. In fact, a yard, which is often protected by walls or sheltering boundaries, can be warm as toast when basking in a benign late-season sun, and there is nothing better than a mid-morning cup of coffee outside on a crisp day, when the temperature can rise surprisingly. A successful yard therefore offers a positive welcome at any time of the year. This is largely due both to a sensitive landscape treatment and a positive melding of house and garden. It is also pretty obvious that if spaces flow together, one helps the other feel larger.

To reinforce the bond between inside and out, we can use a wide range of materials and surfaces, each of which has different characteristics. As we naturally move from the house into the yard, it can make good sense to use compatible materials to reinforce the transition. These can include floor and wall surfaces, as well as color, planting, and even water. I have designed yards using all these features – a crisp slate floor continuing as paving outside; exposed brick walls flowing almost uninterrupted past plate glass sliding doors; pots bursting with foliage in both the living room and yard; and a linear pool running beneath the glass to provide dramatic spatial linkage.

The major hard landscape element in most yards is paving of some kind. This can be slabs, bricks, decking, gravel, cobblestones, or a good few other things. It is worth reiterating that this is where you will spend a good slice of your budget, so it makes sense to get it right first time – mistakes can be expensive. Materials can be grouped into two broad sections – naturally occurring and artificial – and as a general rule the former are the most

expensive. A choice should never be made randomly, and the house should always be the starting point that suggests a theme. Just occasionally the answer is obvious; a fine old natural stone floor, for example, could simply be continued out into the yard. The same might apply to terracotta tiles used in a kitchen or conservatory, these forming a perfect exterior floor with a Mediterranean feel. Just be aware that tiles and certain bricks may not be frostproof, so check with the supplier first. More often than not, though, there may be no obvious link, although the style and construction of the house itself may suggest a theme. If it is built from brick, a similar paving brick could be incorporated in the terrace or patio. Similarly, a wooden house would be perfectly complemented by a deck.

As a general rule, a single paving material, except in a very small space, tends to look a little heavy. Three materials, on the other hand, are invariably too busy on the eye. Two compatible surfaces are often just right – brick

providing a visual link with a similarly built house, teamed with natural stone or good-quality precast concrete slabs can be ideal, for example. Usually, one of the surfaces will be dominant, the brick perhaps being used as courses or panels to frame a larger area of stone.

A little visual manipulation can also help foster the link between inside and out. Often the glimpse of a focal point set some distance away can draw our eye directly into the yard, which is why you should always check the sight lines from doors and windows when working out the initial design. Rather more subtle, but very effective, is to manipulate the floor covering inside to link with a paving pattern outside. I have painted a colored slash across a board floor that ran from inside to out to continue as a similarly colored deck pattern. More expensive, but nonetheless effective, was a blue insert within a striking yellow carpet that turned into a dazzling sweep of sparkling blue glass beads, set within a very crisp contemporary paved terrace. These treatments are a little unusual, but they serve to illustrate the very real advantage of leading the eye from inside to out and in the process maximizing space.

Walls may also offer an opportunity for linking. In urban yards, as in many country gardens, it is quite common for a boundary wall to run directly out from the house. If such a wall adjoins French doors or a picture window, you have the opportunity of extending an interior color scheme outside by painting the wall, providing an obvious and natural link. Yet another practical device is to construct overhead beams that run out from the house over an exterior sitting area. Not only will this reinforce the link between inside and out, it will also frame a view of the space in the garden beyond it. Beams can also help screen obtrusive views into your yard from neighboring upstairs windows; achieving privacy is a key factor in the design of many an urban yard.

left Simplicity in design is everything, but this never precludes subtlety. There is an elegant purity of line here that frames the reflective pool, echoing the sky above.

below right Gates naturally draw both feet and eye to a positive tension point; if they are open, they also provide a view to the next room. Here the fence on each side is also relatively low, so the planting is an additional attractive factor, drawing you forward.

above right The division of space is a great device to use in any yard, and small ones in particular can benefit enormously from the mystery it creates. Walls provide great visual stability, framing a view and demanding that you pass through the gap to explore. The strong shadows that the walls cast also help to divide the area.

dividing up the space

Depending upon where you divide any space, inside or outside the house, you create both separate areas and an opportunity to provide "rooms" of different proportions. A simple rectangle divided in the middle creates two similar spaces, whereas a division two-thirds of the way down offers a quite different feel. A longer space might be divided more often, with the potential to theme each area separately, creating interest. The way in which the ingredients of tension, mystery, and surprise in divided space work is simple, yet essential to a successful design. Imagine a yard divided centrally with two wings of trellis that form a gap in the middle. As you approach the gap, there is first a feeling of mystery as you wonder just what lies beyond; next there is a feeling of tension, at its highest as you pass between the divider; and finally there is the element of surprise as a whole new view opens up.

What the divider is made from matters little: it could be walling, hedging, or loose planting. Each of these will have their own character, cost implications, and theme, which will in turn link them back into the style of yard you have designed. In a tiny yard, it might be a single wing of trellis accessed by a path leading into the hidden space, terminating at a concealed seat or sitting area. This could be looking across rather than down the yard, perhaps focusing on some kind of wall-mounted feature or a fine plant. By positioning a simple screen, a secret sitting area, a cross axis, and a focal point are all created, and the yard has come to life.

A single screen or wing draws attention to one side of a yard; screens from either side, placed at the same distance from the house with a gap in the middle, suggest formality; while staggered dividers allow you to move down the space in a zigzag pattern. Each of these provides different design criteria and possibilities while fulfilling the same basic design function of dividing up the space into interesting parts.

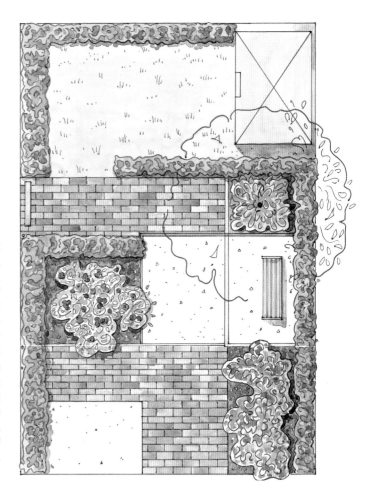

sweeping curves

Any of the four design styles can be adopted when dividing up a garden space. The important thing is that a division should be placed with sensitivity, providing a definite contribution to the overall scheme rather than an ill-conceived barrier around which you have to pass. Both these diagrams suggest ideas rather than complete designs and can be modified to suit your own particular requirements. This one above is built up from strong flowing curves, the hedges sweeping you through the yard with a real feeling of movement. There is a great strength here, one shape interlacing with the next to allow the view to unfold as you move through the space.

geometric progression

This is an asymmetrical design and might form the basis for a secluded front yard. Here hedges overlap with one another, and the route from gate to house is full of interest and surprise. On entering the yard from the street, your eye is drawn to a tree that acts as a focal point, and this naturally turns you through ninety degrees toward the building. The view from the building is altogether different. Here you have a controlled and enclosed space with room for both paving and planting. Some people ignore the possibilities of a front yard, lavishing all their attention at the rear of the house, but it can be a valuable space.

right Containment is a natural function of any yard, and this one demonstrates that the simple approach often works best. Boundary walls provide seclusion and shelter, as well as an excellent background for plants.

the boundaries

One device that has a real visual impact is the way we handle the color, construction, and planting of the boundaries of the yard. The easiest way to think of outdoor boundaries is like the walls of a room inside the house. If you have a bold, heavily patterned wallpaper that draws the eye, the room tends to feel smaller. If, on the other hand, you use a pale colored, delicate pattern, quite the opposite happens, and the area seems larger. In our outside room, the principle is exactly the same. A boundary that is made from a fence with broad slats is dominant and tends to press in on you. Narrow slats tend to refract light, and the fence is less obtrusive. Color is also important here, especially as so many people paint walls or boundaries white in a small yard. White is a reflector that bounces light back at you and can again make a space feel smaller. The successful visual expansion of a space is often better achieved with the use of a color that recedes from the eye. This problem with white or very light shades also explains why new fences, which are often impregnated with a pale colored preservative, are so glaring. Tone them down so light is absorbed rather than reflected, and they will not attract so much attention from the eye.

In a smaller yard, slatted fences, or even trellis, can allow a glimpse of planting next door, immeasurably increasing a feeling of additional space. In such a case, paint the fence dark brown, or even black, so it will simply merge into planting. It is useful at this stage to point out that large leaves on a boundary, like large patterns on wallpaper, are visually demanding and foreshorten the space. Conversely, fine, feathery foliage, like grass, bamboo, and other delicate planting, breaks light up and encourages a feeling of depth. This provides a fascinating insight into how we can control and manipulate space; it would seem that our small and uncompromising yard has all kinds of possibilities.

The smaller a yard, the more important the boundaries become, not just in terms of enclosure, but in offering vertical space for a whole range of features as well. In fact, a tiny yard may well have a greater area of wall space than floor. Very often such space is poorly utilized, but has huge potential for fragrant climbing plants and all kinds of possibilities, ranging from water spouting into bowls, window and wall boxes, to overhead beams or arbors. Think what you can do inside with color, pictures, and ornamentation, and then transfer those same ideas outside and see what a little lateral thinking might achieve.

In many a city courtyard, high walls soar above the more intimate garden space, bringing a real feeling of claustrophobia. Very often these walls are dark brick, which makes the overall picture even more somber. The secret here, and an idea I have used many times, is to make the space more intimate by painting the surrounding walls a pale color up to a point just above doors and windows, usually about 10 feet high. This helps define the yard, drawing the eye down and detracting from the height of the buildings above. Overhead beams running out from the house at the same height will reinforce this feeling of intimacy and may well provide dappled shade and privacy.

While a plain paint scheme is fine, possibly linking with a color or colors from inside the house, why not think a little farther and paint, or have painted, climbers, flower and foliage? Such murals have been used from time immemorial and can either stand alone or act as a foil to real planting. Some purists may balk at this approach, but it can be invaluable in a tiny yard floored with concrete, where vegetation is simply impossible.

If you cannot plant into the ground, or even if you can, wall-hung containers have terrific potential. The larger the growing space in a container the better, affording ample root run and rather less watering than for a smaller pot. Just what you choose is down to personal preference, but the possibilities are endless, as a visit to any garden center will bear witness. Once you have made that choice, think about the pattern of wall-hung containers that you will create: the relationship of pictures on walls inside is no different to their equivalents outside. Look at the wall or boundary as a canvas and arrange its decoration accordingly. The composition could be a formal one with regularly positioned containers; asymmetric with larger items balancing a greater number of smaller ones; or simply a single whopping wall-hung pot as a major focal point for the whole yard. Start the design process with empty rather than full containers and lay them out on the ground in the pattern they are to make. This way, you can juggle positions until you are happy with the end result.

In my own gardens I often build up an eclectic collection of items that can include all kinds of things from plants, plaques, shells, and other found objects. One of the best was a half-basket full of trailing pelargoniums that I surrounded with a large white picture frame. The end result really was dramatic and gave the basket a terrific focus. Windowsills ask for troughs or other containers, not just at ground-floor level but at upstairs windows too. Sills and balconies dripping with flowers and foliage can do much to relieve a dull urban scene, but make sure the boxes or pots are well secured.

right Just how you enclose your yard can have real design repercussions. This boundary simply launches itself up the slope with explosive visual power – an extreme treatment, but a dynamic and successful one.

designing with space

A quite different, but nonetheless important, principle of enclosure can be used where a sitting area adjoins the wider yard. It is a simple fact that when a terrace extends out from the house without any division from the lawn or area beyond, you tend to feel vulnerable when sitting there. This is pure psychology, and it could be argued that it dates back to pre-history when our ancestors surrounded themselves with a stockade as protection from the wild. In our safe contemporary garden environments, we still value shelter and the secure feeling that it creates. It is comfortable to wrap a sitting space about with low, fragrant planting that allows a view out to the garden over the top, but offers a degree of visual containment. Such things are reassuring, and that is what a yard, however large or small, is all about. Even in a great Renaissance garden, there was usually a carefully conceived secret area, where the family could withdraw to, hidden somewhere in the design. The scale of gardening may have changed, but the philosophy is much the same.

Another useful device to make a certain space private and secure is dividing off a paved area or terrace that runs across the rear of a house. Sometimes paving in a yard may constitute the whole thing; instead of just one large area, it may be attractive to divide the space by some kind of feature running out from the house. This could be a raised bed of herbs, which would be both fragrant and practical close to the kitchen. Again, this low planting will wrap around you rather than break the sight lines across the area. The use of overhead beams or an archway might, alternatively, offer both a focused view across the back of the house and create a tension point as you move from space to space.

a miniature yard

This tiny yard, set in the heart of an English country town, is the epitome of sensitive spatial relationships. It is a highly stylized design, with a dominant central axis that leads your eye directly through the wrought-iron gates to the urn and statue beyond. These serve as the major focal point of the yard. On each side, planting softens the strong perspective, slowing the eye by adding its own delicate counterpoint.

1 Stone cherub 2 Wall climbers
3 Gothic screens 4 Urns on piers
5 Spiral box bushes 6 Large planter
7 Mixed planting 8 Freestanding chairs
9 Light fixtures 10 Table
11 Laburnum tree 12 Classical urn
13 Birdbath 14 Wrought-iron gates
15 Large planted urn
16 Blue stable paving stones

a dining area

Eating is a practical business, so if you are going to eat outside, the area you choose needs to cater for its prime function. This does not mean that it cannot be neat or elegant, but this is one place where form really should follow function. How many times, for example, has a meal outside been spoiled by a chilly wind or the glare of a merciless sun on white furniture or walls? The point is that many of us prefer to eat outside in the fresh air, but only if the dining area is comfortable.

To see how outside dining rooms work at their best, look at street cafés, preferably in Europe. You will notice that they have a number of characteristics in common. The prime requisite is shelter, which is then tempered either by shade or warmth. Your favorite restaurant will probably have either generous awnings or overhead screens that shade or gently filter sunlight into delicate patterns that swing across your table as you linger over that last crumb of cake or fine wine. Visit this same place later in the year, or even in winter, and you may well find warming outside heaters or even clear screens that can be dropped down at the first hint of inclement weather. Added to these comforts is ease of access from inside and, perhaps most important of all, a straightforward route from the kitchen.

All of this makes pretty good sense and contains the kind of measured thought that is the basis of a sound yard design. These commercial examples suggest that an outdoor dining area should usually adjoin the house, be positioned close to the kitchen, and have adequate shelter. In fact, these three criteria are the natural ingredients of many patios, which makes them such ideal outside rooms.

We love eating outside, so when we first moved in, I made sure new French doors opened straight out from the kitchen onto a paved area of adequate size. The size

left If you only have limited space, your eating area should be neat yet practical. Here there is a small table and several chairs, the slats of which echo the deck, and wraparound planting – perfect!

is desperately important, because you cannot enjoy a meal in cramped conditions. I hate those parties where you have to mince around with plate and glass with nowhere to put either – or your behind. Our dining area measures a full 18 x 21 feet, which is ample room for table, chairs, and plenty of people. It has three raised beds 18 inches high on which we can perch if necessary and a built-in barbecue against the boundary wall. All of this took a bit of thought, involved a degree of structural alteration, and cost money, but it is worth it because it really works.

We do not have overhead screens, because certain members of our family have a dislike of wildlife dropping into the salad, but we do have one of those whopping parasols, which really is practical since it can be moved around to provide shade where needed. Our latest investment is a portable exterior heater that looks like a floor lamp. These may not be the prettiest things in the world, but they are brilliant, particularly when the barbecue is dying down and that chill night air is creeping in. Their only downside is inducing a willingness

of you or your guests to consume several more bottles of wine before weaving to bed!

One point that many people tend to forget is the kind of paving or surfacing used for the floor. I am a messy chef, and it gets worse as the evening wears on, with dressings, oil, and other ingredients flying around. Natural stone, which costs a fortune, is not good in such places since it stains readily and they are almost impossible to remove. Brick is often a good choice, while many good precast concrete slabs or brushed aggregate surfaces can be easily washed down. This is all part of the practicality of a space that has eating as its prime function. All you need is a quiet design background that can be brought to life with people, cheerful tablecloths, bright colors, music, and good conversation – *bon appétit*!

above Good design often seems almost unconscious. Here sheltering walls, a floating overhead screen that filters strong sun, a simple floor, and, most important of all, a good-sized table to seat plenty of hungry people all come together effortlessly.

left This dining area is supremely functional, with plenty of space that is both easily cleaned down and elegant. Pots provide instant color, while the more distant planting beckons you into the wider outdoors.

changing levels

If all yards were flat, they would be easy to build but relatively less interesting. Changes of level, whether complex or simple, can add immeasurably to the character of a yard, since there are ways in which to capitalize on a slope. In very basic visual terms, an area that slopes up from the house or main viewpoint tends to be foreshortened, while a yard that drops away has the opposite effect, feeling slightly larger. In reality, by the time a yard is furnished with various features, planting, and dividers, this optical effect is virtually eliminated, except in extreme circumstances.

A simple approach to design almost invariably works best, and in a small sloping yard changes in level should be broad and generous. If the space is suitable for division into rooms, each area might occupy its own terrace, accessed by steps. Such changes in level will heighten the elements of tension, mystery, and surprise, since the act of negotiating steps increases concentration and allows views, however small or intimate, to unfold in an altogether more dramatic way.

wraparound steps

Subtlety of design should extend throughout the yard and certainly include the style of any changes in level. Materials adopted in the main paved areas set a theme that can be extended to all parts of the composition. As part of a strong architectural setting, steps should be crisply detailed, and they can often wrap themselves around a change of level forming a right angle. This consequently allows access from two directions, offering a more easygoing and generous ascent.

These steps are unashamedly contemporary, made from a combination of wooden and metal strips, which are also used elsewhere in the yard. Such a design runs the risk of becoming clinical, but the deft touch of a cutout area of chips and sprawling thymes offers a clever and successful counterpoint to the austerity of wood and metal.

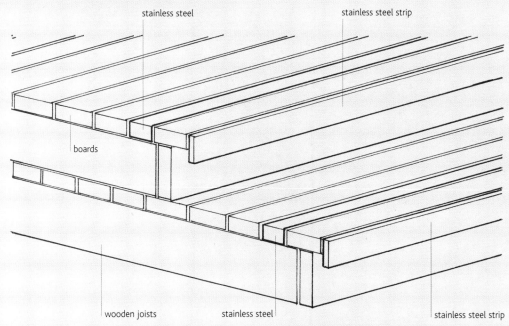

stainless steel

stainless steel strip

boards

wooden joists

stainless steel

stainless steel strip

As a general rule, there is nothing worse than small, narrow steps, so think of making them as wide as sensibly possible so they can double as places for pots or statuary. Steps make great occasional seats and if they are big enough, they can cater for party people without the clutter of too many tables and chairs. Plan steps to become part of the overall floorscape, extending a paving pattern and matching materials used elsewhere in the composition.

With a gentle slope, steps may extend the whole width of a yard, but if the climb is steeper, they may not be so wide and may rise through or alongside a retaining wall. The latter is simply a support to hold the upper level in place and naturally needs to be strongly built with

above Here steps and deck blend into an integrated whole, providing a real feeling of continuity. The slight overhang creates an attractive shadow, and the fern softens the end of this generous change of level.

left Changes of direction can add immeasurably to the character of a flight of steps. These cleverly supported treads almost float up the slope, disappearing with an air of mystery that encourages you to explore farther.

below "Concrete is the stone of the twentieth century," said architect Frank Lloyd Wright. This clever detail incorporates a planting strip at the rear of each concrete tread that naturally softens the flight.

or relatively complex, interlocking with steps and planting, or even forming a complete water stair, skittering from one level to another down its own steps.

There is often a temptation, particularly in very small yards, to construct steep steps, simply because they are perceived to take up less space. With a little design ingenuity you can normally produce an easier flight without diminishing the working area of the yard. Apart from being downright dangerous, steep steps are a chore to negotiate. There is a classic step proportion that has a rise of 6 inches and a tread of 18 inches. This is slightly shallower than a stair inside your home and consequently rather easier going. Although steps have all kinds of possibilities, they pose problems for moving mowers, wheelbarrows, and other heavy equipment. In a tiny yard

suitable foundations. In aesthetic terms, however, a wall can be far more than just that. When working with slopes in my own gardens, I use all kinds of retaining walls to create terraces. Brick, stone, concrete, logs, or railroad ties can all be suitable, but again should carry on the hard landscaping themes used elsewhere in the garden design. When these yards are built and planted, the walls all but disappear beneath a cascade of flowers and foliage, which of course is just as it should be; a change of level is a wonderful vehicle for the softening influence of plants tumbling from above and climbing from below. Water is another great element to introduce into a yard on different levels, dropping from one level to another. Water has the added bonus of sound that helps bring the smallest yard alive. Such a cascade can be simple

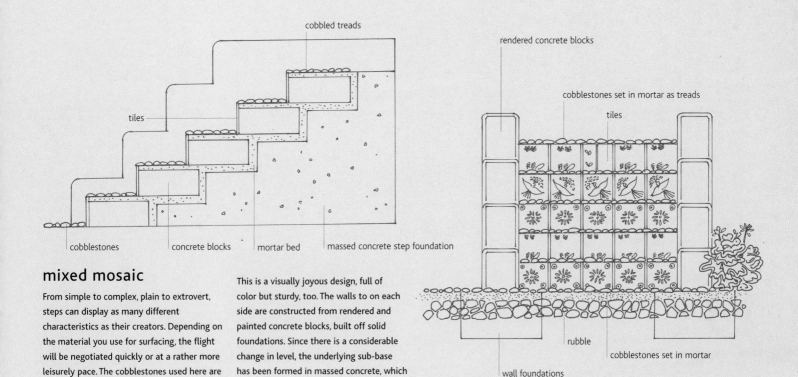

cobbled treads

tiles

cobblestones   concrete blocks   mortar bed   massed concrete step foundation

rendered concrete blocks

cobblestones set in mortar as treads

tiles

rubble

cobblestones set in mortar

wall foundations

mixed mosaic

From simple to complex, plain to extrovert, steps can display as many different characteristics as their creators. Depending on the material you use for surfacing, the flight will be negotiated quickly or at a rather more leisurely pace. The cobblestones used here are slightly uneven and will slow you down.

This is a visually joyous design, full of color but sturdy, too. The walls to on each side are constructed from rendered and painted concrete blocks, built off solid foundations. Since there is a considerable change in level, the underlying sub-base has been formed in massed concrete, which also acts as a buttress to the terrace above.

you may not need such tools, but if you do, a ramp can be invaluable. Ramps take up more horizontal space than steps but can be relatively narrow, as long as there are no sharp turns to negotiate. Be sure to construct them from a nonslip surface such as textured bricks or block or granite, or they will be impossible to use in damp or icy weather.

Level changes need not simply be built up in rectangular patterns, square with the boundaries; they might be curved, hexagonal, or set on the diagonal. All these possibilities are an integral part of the yard design, and a sloping yard might be built up from two or more overlapping shapes. Each module could be part paved, part planted, contain a water feature, seating, and much else, depending on the overall size of the plot.

Some yards are so complicated by different levels or cross falls that they present real problems in both design and visual terms. They can present the perfect situation for laying a series of decks, linked by steps to form platforms on different levels. In a small yard, it will be easy enough to incorporate built-in furniture, planters, and other split-level features, such as water and even a hot tub or Jacuzzi to fit perfectly into the void beneath a deck. In any split-level yard lighting is essential: steps, ramps, and other areas will need good but subtle illumination.

tricking the eye

While even the smallest yard offers enormous enjoyment, it is always a good idea to try to maximize the available space. Sometimes this can be achieved by building space-saving features or extending the floor area, but in the final analysis the size of your yard will always be finite. There is nothing wrong with this, and small is most certainly beautiful in terms of maintenance. However, visual trickery can not only make your yard feel bigger, but it can also be enormous fun. There are numerous optical illusions and devices; although few stand up to close scrutiny, they certainly have their place in the overall design.

The danger is of pretension, and I cannot abide those false-perspective trellises pompously referred to as *trompe l'oeil*. They are usually put in by equally pompous people and focus on some poor classical figure; in short, they fool nobody and do little for the composition as a whole. I have also seen perspective used in small urban spaces where a lawn is narrowed toward one end and pots or plants placed as flanking elements. These may also decrease in size and focus on a statue, arbor, or other focal point at the end of the vista. Such a design can certainly work from the primary viewpoint, but as soon as you walk down the space and look back, the effect is decidedly uncomfortable – the perspective lines are reversed and there is no feeling of receding space at all. Therefore, before you start playing with

visual trickery, be aware of what your are up to and do it with your tongue firmly in your cheek!

Murals have been a part of the garden scene for many thousands of years, and the best are true works of art. When you have walls, the temptation to paint them becomes almost irresistible, but if you think about going down this particular route, the painting should extend the theme of the yard rather than be simply art for art's sake. An Italianate yard could become a cloister with subtly painted arches flanking two sides; a design colleague, for example, created a wonderful Provençal garden with a painted window looking out over painted lavender fields.

We once created a town garden within high oppressive walls and brought the eye down with that trick of painting the lower sections a different color. I then took the idea even farther and painted an imitation brick wall running out from the house. A painted tomcat stalked along the top, picking his way through real climbing plants, heading toward a painted stone stair that dropped into the yard itself. Again, this kind of approach is pure hallucination, but it can bring great style. Painted moon gates in Japanese-inspired gardens and a rendered view of the Manhattan skyline on a New York terrace are both valid, so let your imagination run wild within the context of your yard's particular location.

left A well-positioned window, albeit between two different sections of yard, will naturally frame the view and throw it into sharp perspective. In addition, it urges continued exploration through and into the depths of the yard.

right Mirrors can be great fun and work to increase the apparent size of a yard enormously. The mirror used here is set at an angle to capture a dramatic reflection of planting, resulting in an image that is almost surreal.

There are also all kinds of appliquéd devices that have potential, the best of which are doors and windows. There is nothing more visually irresistible than a partially open door through a wall – where does it go, what does it hide? Of course, it goes nowhere, but a real door hung from a wooden frame with a couple of steps up and pots standing on each side is real enough and does a pretty good job in the deception stakes. A real window frame set into the boundary allows you to paint a view inside, so the side of a factory may appear to have a view over a quite different landscape.

A mirror is another popular device to trick the eye in a small yard, but subtlety must be paramount if the end result is not to be ludicrous. There is little point in positioning a mirror at the end of your path simply to see yourself resolutely marching toward it. The secret is to set a mirror at an oblique angle to the main viewpoint, say the French doors or a seat, so the reflection is directed away from your eye line and takes in a view of a different part of the yard. A clever device, and one that can work well, is to build a false arch in a wall and recess a mirror into it. Group pots and foliage around it, not too many, but enough to trick a visitor into the reality of the situation. Everything on the one side is reflected, and it really can seem as though you are looking into a completely different outdoor room. A mirror-backed window frame set against or into a wall and fronted by a flowerbed has the wonderful effect of seeming to look into a bed beyond, often an easier alternative than painting a scene.

Although there is a special outside grade of mirror glass available, I use pretty much anything that comes to hand. Old dressing mirrors are fine and often quite big, which is useful. Mirror tiles often fit neatly into a window frame or can be used to build up a reflective pattern on any vertical surface. Tiles or a larger mirror can also look great set into the rear of trellis, which can form a wing that helps divide the garden. Mirrors are now also available in silvered polyester sheet or silvered acrylic, both of which are virtually unbreakable and therefore perfectly safe with young children around. If you want some real fun, you could get an old fairground distorting mirror: it will not increase the visual size of your yard, much but it will break the ice at parties. The fact that mirrors lose their silvering after a while really does not matter; when they are partially covered with planting, the image is in any event broken up. It is extremely unlikely, incidentally, that a bird will fly into a mirror that is well disguised with foliage.

A wonderful visual trick that increases the perceived size of a small yard can be achieved by the careful positioning of lights of decreasing size and wattage. If you imagine wall lights or lights set down each side of a path that become slightly smaller and weaker with distance, you can see that at night this will produce a wonderful effect of illuminated false perspective. This often works better than conventional false perspective, since after dark you move around the space rather less and often view the yard from a specific point. So if you have the ability to be clever inside the house, then do the same thing outside and do not be afraid to experiment. You can try most effects before finalizing them, and the yard can easily be rearranged in any event – so never be afraid of trying out interesting ideas.

material world

Time was when choices of material were relatively easy; the reason why so many traditional street scenes or yards look comfortable and harmonious is the fact that they used vernacular materials. Today we are spoiled for choice – but the solution can still be straightforward in visual terms.

Most natural stone paving materials are expensive because they have to be quarried and skillfully sawn or split into manageable sizes. The classic paving in Great Britain is a sandstone known as York stone, although similar sandstones are found worldwide. When bought new it really is expensive, and even secondhand the cost of enough stone for a large area can be prohibitive. In a small yard, however, you might well consider its use. The wonderful thing about natural stone is its subtle variation, both in surface texture and color, so the effect it produces when well laid can be unique. This kind of paving often looks best when it is laid in a random pattern, using rectangular slabs of different sizes. Slate, which can either have a textured or polished surface, can look wonderfully crisp, but may become slippery in wet weather. Crazy paving, with all those conflicting angles, looks busy and uncomfortable close to a house; the prime rule of simplicity applies just as much to details as it does to the overall design.

On a smaller scale, you can obtain cube-shaped granite bricks. These were traditionally used as street paving and are virtually indestructible. Their small size makes them ideal for paving into the awkward shapes characteristic of a courtyard. You will often see them laid in fan or circular patterns, which can add another dimension to their design potential. The only drawback of granite bricks is that they provide a slightly uneven surface, which is not ideal for tables and chairs on a sitting or eating area. Cobblestones are those wonderful egg-shaped, water-worn stones that can either be laid loose, as an excellent ground cover, or bedded in mortar.

The secret with either method is to lay the cobblestones so no soil or mortar is visible. Again the surface is uneven but wonderfully tactile.

Decking can provide a highly versatile exterior floor. It can be quickly laid using long planks to any number of patterns. The secret is to provide ventilation beneath the surface of the wood, otherwise, rot can quickly set in. This means that the top visible surface of the deck needs to be supported in exactly the same way as a floor inside the house, on bearers or joists of some kind. Just occasionally, you may be able to deck over an old paved surface of slabs or cracked concrete, saving a good deal of hard work and subsequent removal of material, which is often a problem in a confined urban yard. There is more to a deck than simply slapping boards down in any old pattern. It has the potential to draw the eye, and if

above This shallow pool is floored with brightly colored tiles to provide a focus, while the surrounding paving is a combination of different tiles and cobblestones that build up a fascinating pattern.

left Grids are the basis of many patterns and can often play with perceptions of perspective. There is a strange interplay here between geometric stability and optical unease, depending on how the eye reads the design.

left Mosaics have a long and distinguished history, but the success of this little pebble vignette lies in its ability to draw the eye and turn the corner of the path. Such features, apart from being highly artistic, can last a lifetime if properly laid.

below Wooden decking has an inherently warm and comfortable feel, and therefore creates an interesting dialogue with the adjoining granite bricks on the lower level. The use of different surfaces indicates a corresponding change of garden function.

There is an even larger selection of manmade materials, the main players including paving slabs made from precast concrete that are relatively cheap and easy to lay. There is an increasingly good choice of slabs that look very like their natural counterparts, but at about half the price. Some are riven to look like old stone, while others are smooth and architectural. Choose and use them in relation to the design you have created.

Brick is one of the most useful pavings of all, and many manufacturers are now producing frostproof "pavoirs" in a huge choice of colors. Brick provides a natural link with a similarly built house or boundary walls and has a wonderfully mellow quality that blends well with planting. The same brick can be used for raised beds, seats, and other built-in features, providing additional continuity throughout the yard.

Always be aware of how a paving pattern can help control space. In a narrow yard, slabs or bricks laid across the area, in a staggered bond, will tend to make it feel wider and therefore bigger. Exactly the same material laid down the yard will do the opposite, leading the eye and making the space feel narrower. Whatever material you use, this same characteristic will be apparent, so use the technique positively to add to your composition.

it is run out directly from the house, a deck offers that inevitable feeling of linkage. Conversely, a diagonal pattern provides diagonal emphasis; and boards laid like tiles in a checkerboard have an altogether more busy visual nature. If you vary board widths, you can set up all kinds of rhythms, while color wisely used can be either dramatic or subtle.

Railroad ties can also be used, either as paving or as raised beds. It is important to make sure they are clean and not soaked with pitch or oil, which can sweat out in hot weather with disastrous results. Ties are heavy and powerful, with a long linear shape; they seem to have a masculine quality that associates well with large-leafed architectural planting and paler hard surfaces such as gravel or chips. Raised beds can be quickly and easily built if the ties are laid like bricks in a wall. Three courses high is usually enough, and the wide outer edges of such a bed will also double as a space-saving seats.

above This simple grid, formed with granite bricks and in-filled with gravel, provides both a frame for planting and a device to lead the eye directly towardsthe steps and upper level.

right If paving is laid with care, in contrasting blocks, sizes, and courses, the end result is a hard-wearing and attractive exterior carpet. Here simple raised beds, planting, boulders, and cobblestones enhance the effect and make a fascinating textural pattern.

color, pattern, and texture

While the role of color, pattern, and texture of plants in bringing the garden alive is taken for granted, it is often overlooked in terms of hard surfacing. In fact, the way in which we choose and use flooring of various kinds can make a huge difference to the way we perceive and move around a yard. Smooth surfaces encourage speed, while textured paving slows you down a little, and gravels and chips reduce movement even more. Uneven cobblestones need careful negotiation, while full-blown boulders stop you dead.

The type of paving we lay tends to control movement, something I learned early in my own garden. In the small front yard, I had eliminated car parking and opted for a low-maintenance composition of paving, planting, and large smooth boulders. The latter were wonderfully sculptural, associating perfectly with bold, largely evergreen shrubs. The natural route from street to front door was in a diagonal line, across a crisp combination of pale-colored precast paving slabs and brick that provided a visual link with the building. Such a smooth surface encouraged a brisk footfall, and every day the postman stepped smartly toward the mailbox, stamping unceremoniously on a prize hosta. It was clear that his route was the shortest distance, so I repositioned a number of my smooth boulders adjacent to the suffering specimen. The next morning my postman headed along his usual route and caught his ankle a terrific blow. Needless to say, he never stood on the hosta again!

left In a modern context, paving can be equally contemporary, and at last designers are starting to use the materials at their disposal in thoroughly innovative ways. Here decking is combined with steel strips and stepping stones planted with thyme that offer a fascinating counterpoint.

right Weight of materials is an important consideration when designing a roof terrace, and this is where synthetic materials, including plastic, can come into their own. This roof is pure boisterous fun, with the different-colored polka dots setting up their own rhythms as they dance across the surface.

a modern art

Although the modern movement developed early in the twentieth century, its principles have stood the test of time, illustrated here in a thoroughly contemporary garden. The fascination of modern art lies in a celebration of geometry where contrasting shapes, volumes, colors, and often textures combine to form perfectly balanced compositions. Such design is based on asymmetry, in which a delicacy of balance is all-important. In the garden planned and pictured here, there is a wonderful interplay of spatial relationships and surfaces – water, walls, color, and minimal planting combining to produce pure art. In Britain we are often obsessed with flower and foliage, which can dull our sense of space. This composition is a lesson in design that can persuade you to pare away any such lingering sentimentality.

1 Deciduous trees with light foliage
2 Steps between levels
3 High walls, retaining and as screen across yard 4 Gravel flooring
5 Area of planting 6 Raised pool crossing over levels

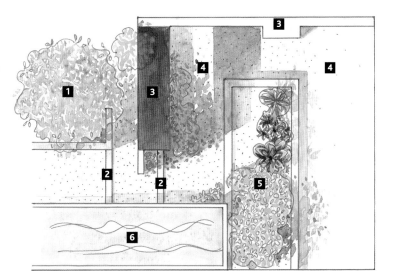

While yards can provide the most wonderfully intimate spaces, they can also, if surrounded by high walls, be relatively dark. There are all kinds of ways you can counter this, but one of the best is by using a pale-colored floor that will help reflect available light. Paving comes in a wide choice of colors and some of them are helpfully pale. Larger rather than smaller slabs tend to look just a little brighter, since there are fewer joints to absorb light. A word of warning here; while pale cream or gray slabs are fine, avoid colored paving like the plague, since it often fades to a sickly hue and is far too brash. Any paved surface should provide a quiet background on which all kinds of activities can take place

White or plain colored stone chips can be genuinely useful, particularly in very dark situations, such as basement courts in the middle of town. They can be laid either as a complete floor covering, with plants growing through and stepping stones for access, or as a counterpoint to other materials. A sharp contrast, such as black slate or a dark paving, can be dramatic. Try "sliding" one surface against another with paving jutting out into the chips to provide real visual contrast.

The opposite situation is a bright, light yard or roof terrace that basks in full sun. Rather than using white, tone things down with wonderful terracotta and earthy hues that soak up rather than reflect light. In strong sun, beware of dark paving, which can become unbearably hot to bare feet. Wood is wonderful in such circumstances, and decks are both practical and good looking, harking back to their California roots. This is where genuine Spanish patios and Mediterranean yards provide inspiration: in the right situation, rough plastered walls, crudely fashioned overheads smothered with fragrant climbers, and richly patterned or terracotta tiles on the floor will look perfect. Add a simple wall-mounted water feature, with that delicious sound on a hot summer's day, and you are as close to heaven as you are likely to get. The best of such yards are never contrived, but the brighter and nearer the equator you get, the more color, pattern, and texture a yard can accept without seeming busy. This is all due to light; the stronger it is, the more it tones down both visual and human activity.

Designers are increasingly exploring all kinds of different new materials, from glass to plastic, and although many people have difficulty in accepting them, they really can have terrific potential. Glass is becoming particularly popular and is available in a whole number of guises from crushed, with safely rounded edges, to florists' beads. Its main characteristic is its ability to sparkle in sunlight or reflect any available light in dark places. There are many colors of glass on the market, ranging from bright primary hues right down to muted pastels. I use glass for all kinds of outdoor applications, from top-dressing the soil around plants in pots to surrounding shimmering stainless-steel water features. At their most dramatic, glass beads can form great sweeps of sparkling color as a substitute lawn; or they can be used in much the same way as gravel, as a wonderful foil for plants that are positioned to grow through the surface.

A little farther along the way of contemporary design is plastic. For years Astroturf, or artificial grass, has been used in all kinds of situations and is available in a whole range of colors. The problem arises when people think of it as aping grass, when in fact they should really be using the surface as a low-maintenance carpet. Its potential is considerable, being light- and rot-proof, so use your imagination to create sweeps, swirls, or patterns that link one with another and even perhaps with an internal color scheme. Industrial flooring has huge potential and can be obtained in fantastic colors with textured surfaces to prevent slipping. Plastics warm up quickly but do not become too hot; they can be laid, like carpet or vinyl flooring, up and down slopes, eliminating steps and preventing weed growth. I have even used woven polyester as lightweight fencing and internal garden screens, stretched between equally light alloy frameworks. There is a huge palette of materials out there, but we often lack the imagination or perhaps the courage to exploit it. Try some of these possibilities; you could be wonderfully surprised by the results.

blueprints
for furnishing

above This scene is just delicious, tucked into a corner with definite Japanese overtones. There is a solidity and permanence in stone that is perfectly complemented by the simple slatted fence and planting.

right Yards are primarily about relaxation – restful rooms outside. Built-in seating is not only comfortable, but also saves valuable space. When it is allied to a very personal style of exterior decoration, it makes your yard unique.

creative design is underpinned by practicality. All the carefully planned furnishings, features, and surfaces will need good and careful construction for the yard to look good. Whether you carry out the work yourself or have a reputable contractor do it for you, high standards and attention to detail are always paramount. The success of any feature depends upon the things you cannot see – the foundations, sub-base, and mechanics. The principle is the same for outdoor hard landscaping as it is when wallpapering a wall: if the preparation is poor, the end result looks awful and will quickly deteriorate. Similarly, if pumps and equipment are poorly installed or lack sufficient power, water features will underperform; and lighting also need special care and installation.

Paved surfaces that form the base and background for furnishing should always be laid to a slight slope away from the house and should be 6 inches beneath any dampproofing. Many yards surrounded by walls and largely floored with paving can collect rainwater alarmingly quickly, so one or more drains will be an absolute necessity. Paving can then be sloped toward them accordingly. Walls – boundary, dividers, or raised features – should always be built on sound foundations twice as wide as the wall itself. The depth of foundations depends on the underlying soil, and they should normally be taken down to undisturbed ground. Although this is common sense, it is amazing how often it is lacking – with dire consequences!

A worthwhile end result need not necessarily cost a huge amount of money. We have been exhorted to buy brandnew materials and larger plants in a vain attempt to create an instant garden, but increasingly this view is being reversed. Gardening has never been a quick fix, nor should it be. Half the fun is in watching a garden develop, modifying and adding elements as you go. Like the people who make them, all gardens are different and each will respond to different treatment. Patios are naturally small, intimate places that need not consume huge amounts of material. I have known yards where virtually all the bricks, paving slabs, fencing, and lumber have been quite literally found, taken home, and used. Such yards almost inevitably look instantly mature and comfortable – a real bonus for any outside room.

living outside

Relaxation comes high on the garden design list. There needs to be ample room for sitting, eating, and general inactivity. In this delightful outdoor room, all of these elements are carefully considered. Overheads filter sun and provide dappled shade, steps, and low retaining walls offer a casual perching place and conventional benches, tables, and chairs complete the picture.

1 Shed 2 Freestanding bench 3 Boundary wall 4 Mixed planting 5 Brick paving 6 Decorated tiles 7 Mosaic steps 8 Cobblestones 9 Miniature pool 10 Decking 11 Larger pool 12 Containers 13 Overhead beams 14 Utility area

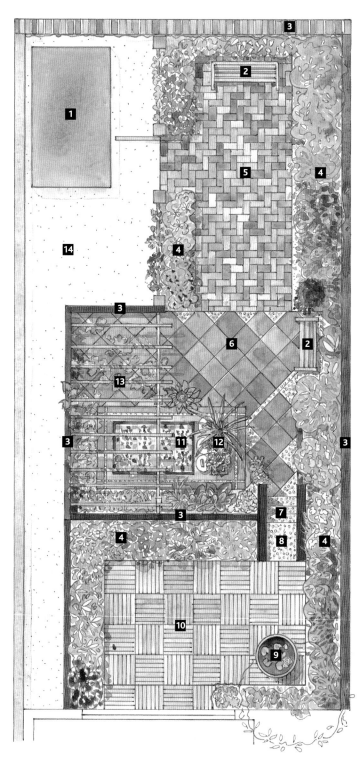

outdoor furniture

With the feeling of intimacy and shelter of a small garden space comes relaxation. With a yard's close physical links to the house, sitting, eating, and general basking become second nature, but to do these comfortably we need to think about its furnishings. Space is at a premium, so ways to build and arrange furniture in the most efficient yet visually attractive way are essential. If features can have a dual role – a raised bed doubling as a seat or a built-in barbecue counter with room for potted plants – then so much the better.

As is the case inside the home, the style chosen for the outdoor furnishings can make or break a composition. It need not rigidly adhere to a particular design idiom; for example, I have seen traditional, formal gardens successfully equipped with stunning contemporary furniture and ornaments. Conversely, the most avant-garde yard may have a glorious classical urn as a major focal point. Provided the underlying design is positive and has integrity, the overlay of furnishing can either follow suit or be entirely eclectic.

below There is a wonderfully original juxtaposition here between the trees and soft woodland planting and the crisp hard landscape beyond. The latter forms a compact yet elegant sitting area surrounded by a contemporary moat.

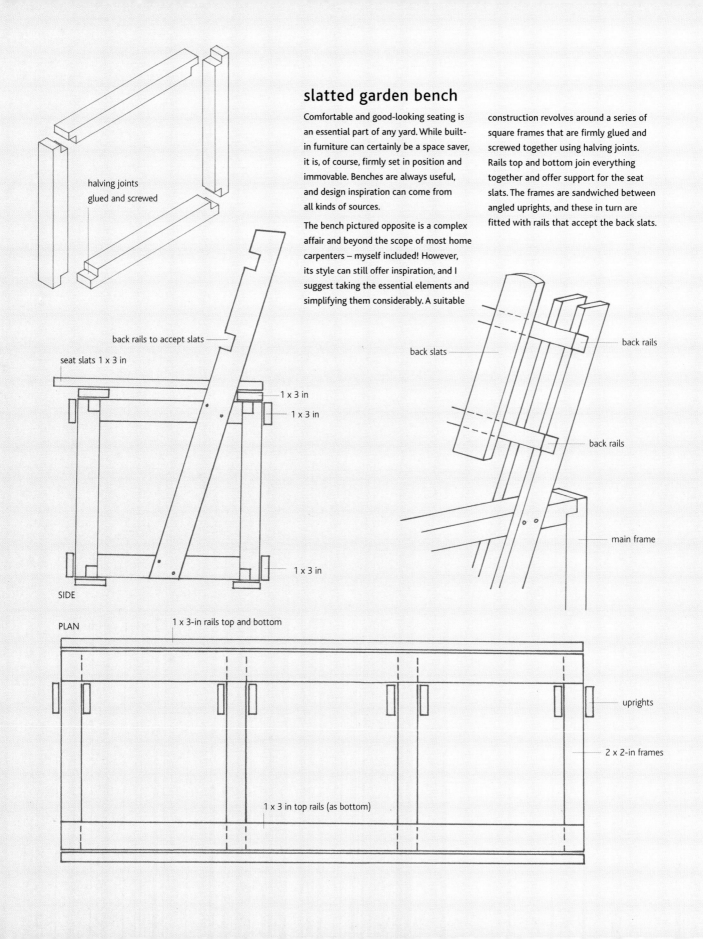

halving joints
glued and screwed

slatted garden bench

Comfortable and good-looking seating is an essential part of any yard. While built-in furniture can certainly be a space saver, it is, of course, firmly set in position and immovable. Benches are always useful, and design inspiration can come from all kinds of sources.

The bench pictured opposite is a complex affair and beyond the scope of most home carpenters – myself included! However, its style can still offer inspiration, and I suggest taking the essential elements and simplifying them considerably. A suitable

construction revolves around a series of square frames that are firmly glued and screwed together using halving joints. Rails top and bottom join everything together and offer support for the seat slats. The frames are sandwiched between angled uprights, and these in turn are fitted with rails that accept the back slats.

back rails to accept slats

seat slats 1 x 3 in

1 x 3 in

1 x 3 in

1 x 3 in

SIDE

back slats

back rails

back rails

main frame

PLAN

1 x 3-in rails top and bottom

uprights

2 x 2-in frames

1 x 3 in top rails (as bottom)

sitting and cooking outside

Much of the space in a yard will be multifunctional, but eating and entertaining usually come pretty high on the agenda. Space is usually needed for table, chairs, and often a barbecue, which more often than not becomes a focus to the place. The whole cooking and dining area, if possible, should be no less than 12 feet square, which equates pretty well to an average dining room inside the house. A little space will obviously be saved if furniture is built in, but on the other hand, a freestanding table and chairs can be moved around to chase sun or shade. Chairs need to be chosen with care; sit before you buy, as what looks elegant may be appallingly uncomfortable. Some manufacturers are slowly becoming more aware of posture and ergonomics, but many still have little idea of these concerns. The worst offenders are perhaps the imitation wrought-iron chairs that are likely both to wobble and to leave a lasting floral imprint on your backside!

Depending on where you live, some kind of overhead structure can be useful to protect from sun or light rain. Hot countries embrace the veranda, which is one of the more civilized inventions, providing a wonderful transitional link between inside and out. Awnings can be effective and have the added advantage of being rolled away when not wanted; and overhead beams with fragrant climbers or a vine can be the perfect antidote to sun in a hot climate. Large parasols are becoming increasingly popular, but I never quite know what to do with the things when they are folded up.

Fire has been the hub of encampments since the earliest of times, and the barbecue continues in this tradition pretty well. Both built-in and portable models have advantages, but more important is their size — they really do have to be large enough for a decent amount of food. If you opt for a built-in barbecue, site it sensibly away from windows and back it against a

left This rather elegant seat is beyond home construction, but it offers both a focal point and room for a good few people. A nice touch is the comfortable backrest, and the tree above will create dappled shade – always welcome on a hot day.

right Practicality is the name of the game here with ample work surface and a barbecue slotted into the neat recess. Overhead beams provide shade to the dining area below, and I particularly like the storage area that can accommodate anything from logs to gas bottles.

rectangular tree seat

I like my garden features to work hard for a living, yet to be practical and simple. A tree is a natural focus, and a large platform around it can play a number of parts – as a seat, play surface, and generous table. I am fond of rectangular structures, since they are easy on the eye and straightforward to make.

For this tree seat I have used lumber throughout, the strong legs either concreted into the ground or placed on stone pads, which need to be absolutely level. Cross-pieces brace everything together and act as supports for the top slats, which are cut and fitted around the tree bole. Side slats are easily attached, and for durability I always use brass screws rather than nails.

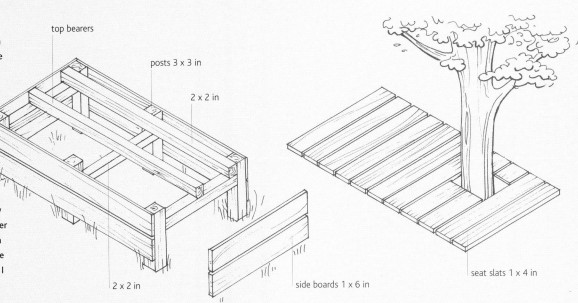

top bearers

posts 3 x 3 in

2 x 2 in

2 x 2 in

side boards 1 x 6 in

seat slats 1 x 4 in

home cooking

This is my own barbecue design, which I have built for dozens of clients. Brick is a strong and versatile material, and construction is straightforward, adaptable enough to fit in virtually any situation. Such a barbecue sits comfortably against a wall, and metal strips can be built into the brickwork to support the charcoal tray and cooking grid. A countertop is essential and can also form the roof of a storage area for tools and equipment. An adjoining built-in seat completes the picture.

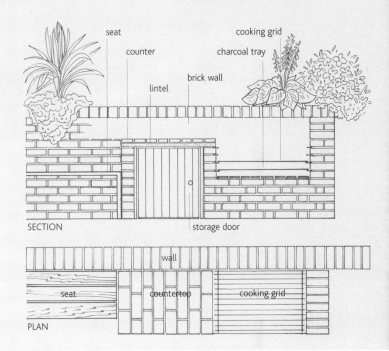

boundary wall or a freestanding wall, which could become a divider within the overall garden pattern. Most of the barbecues we design have the cooking grid to one side, a countertop adjoining, and a built-in seat alongside. The whole arrangement often fits neatly into the right angle formed by two walls. Underneath the countertop, a built-in cupboard for tools, equipment, or children's toys is useful, as storage space is at a premium in most yards.

Winter is not normally the season for alfresco eating, and a built-in barbecue can look decidedly dreary. It may fit neatly into the angle of walls, and if it is wood you can block the front in, hinge the top, and provide useful storage. Seats can also be hinged down from a wall or divider, saving space when they are stored vertically. It can be a good idea to have a deep tray made to replace the charcoal tray when not in use. This can be planted with winter-flowering species. Alternatively, a group of pots on the counter or along the backing wall will help to brighten up the scene.

raised features

Raised features, such as beds or pools, can double as occasional seats, ideally at a height of 18 inches. The finish is important: single brick on edge coping is adequate, but can be slightly uncomfortable; a better detail would be a two-brick-wide coping, and a bull-nosed, rounded edge is particularly suitable. Alternatively, use a smooth paving slab or natural stone coping, and remember that cushions will take off any chill and add a touch of color.

Decking is perhaps the ultimate, versatile material for building in features and furnishings. In a steeply sloping small yard, the upper section of a deck can double as a seat, and others can be built around trees or larger shrubs. You can buy very expensive tree seats, more often than not circular or hexagonal in shape, and in a small rectangular space such forms can be visually uncomfortable. However, it is not difficult or expensive to purposely-build around a tree a rectangular seat that is big enough to double as a low table or even as a play surface. Decking can also be used for other garden features, such as walkways or bridges spanning an area of planting, or a pool.

left Rills have one of the longest pedigrees of all garden features; they were used by the Egyptians, Romans, Moors, and virtually everybody since. They can be raised, as in this modern example, or placed at ground level, on one plane or dropping down a slope.

raising the level

Raised beds are not only practical, saving a deal of bending, but also give young plants a boost in height. This is the easiest construction of all, which uses solid concrete blocks built on equally solid foundations. A useful height, as here, is about 2 ft and the bed can be cement rendered and color-washed. Good soil and drainage are vital, so weep-holes should be incorporated at the base of the bed to remove excess water.

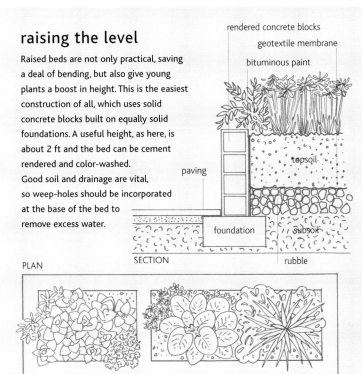

rendered concrete blocks
geotextile membrane
bituminous paint
topsoil
paving
foundation
subsoil
SECTION
rubble
PLAN

bridging space

Bridges are fun, whether they be over a babbling brook or, as here, a dry stream bed. Much of their charm lies in their proximity to another element, heightening your appreciation and also offering a degree of tension.

This bridge is mercifully simple, and its construction is very easy. The two main bearers can be shaped at a lumber yard, and they work to give the feature its curving shape, which visually springs over the gap. Set the ends on solid concrete pads, making sure they are all at the same level. The top boards are simply screwed to the bearers, while boulders and planting bring the whole feature alive.

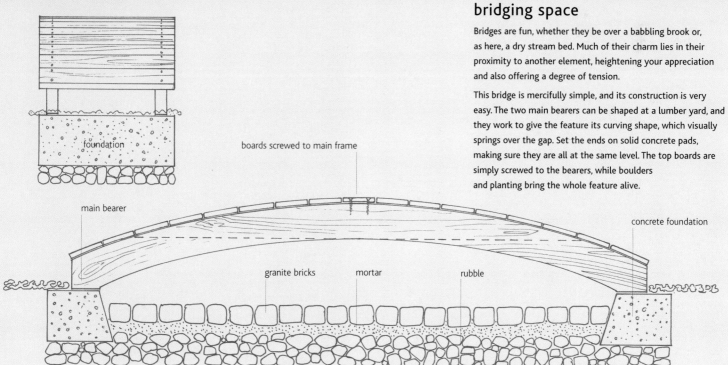

foundation

boards screwed to main frame

main bearer

concrete foundation

granite bricks   mortar   rubble

water features

Of all the elements in a garden, water is perhaps the most enchanting. It can be versatile, subtle, bold, reflective, expansive, or just downright simple. It provides sound and movement, a habitat for fish, plants, and wildlife, and it very often becomes a focus for the whole yard. The eye-catching position of a water feature is important and needs thought at the initial design phase. It could be modern or traditional, but above all else, it will bring the place alive. It will almost certainly be small, since the available space in a yard is not likely to be great.

pools

With the restriction of space, most people will automatically reject open water in favor of a wall-mounted or smaller feature, but I have seen relatively large pools in small yards that have looked fantastic. It all depends on what you want from the space, and if water really turns you on and you are prepared to sacrifice other features or floor area, the results can be spectacular. One great advantage of a pool is reflection, which can bring a whole new dimension of echoed images to the yard. A pool can increase available light with its mirrorlike quality, produce rippling shadow patterns on adjoining walls and offer space for all kinds of aquatic plants and for beautiful waterlily blooms.

A pool can be perfectly still and utterly serene, subtly rippled with a bubble jet, or full of life from a dancing fountain. There is no other garden feature with so many moods, which will change throughout the day and over the entire year with the turning of the seasons. If you have space and a change of level, one pool can tumble or spill into another. Alternatively, a wall-mounted spout could fall to a larger pool below. Shapes, too, are infinitely variable, from simple circles or rectangles to complex geometric patterns – but before you get too excited, remember the relationship of any such shape to the overall yard design.

In practical terms, there are a few sensible things to remember with open water, or with any water feature, for that matter. A pool should be in a light, open position, away from overhanging trees that will drop leaves

right Here is a good design – simple, clean, at odds with, yet reflecting and drawing the landscape in through the reflective pool. Minimal planting respects the immediate surroundings, and although many would call it stark, it has purity.

pond cascade

A water feature such as this can often look complicated, but is really very simple. Its effect is delightful, with water swirling out of an urn into the pool below. The surrounding planting has one of the urns standing among flower and foliage on dry land.

One of the most important factors is to make sure the urns are frostproof, particularly with so much water splashing around. The heart of the system is a submersible pump positioned on a marginal shelf. The urn is supported on concrete blocks or bricks, and the feed pipe taken through the drainage hole in the bottom of the urn. Switch on, and off it goes.

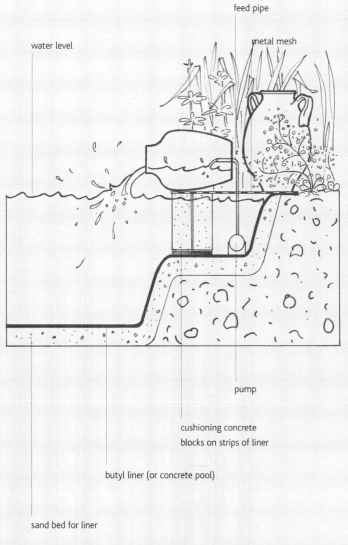

feed pipe

metal mesh

water level

pump

cushioning concrete blocks on strips of liner

butyl liner (or concrete pool)

sand bed for liner

likely to clog pumps and filters. If you are desperate to have a pool and you have trees in the vicinity, cover the area with a thin plastic net in the fall to collect leaves that drop.

No normal garden pool need be more than 24 inches deep and 18 inches is quite adequate. Construction methods vary and are well recorded in specialized watergarden books, but in a small area you can use preformed plastic ponds. They come in all kinds of shapes, but use the larger sizes that give you more room for plants and fish, both of which will not only provide interest, but will also produce a balanced habitat. Tough butyl rubber or plastic laminate is used to make pond liners, which are easy to install and last indefinitely, provided overenthusiastic children do not pierce them with spears or a garden fork. This material can be used for formal or informal shapes; the latter can be ideal in a freeform garden, with a cobblestone or pebble beach providing access for wildlife.

Raised pools can be built in a range of materials that lift the water level to whatever height you want. This might be just 18 inches, to double as an occasional seat, or even higher, incorporating planting in split-level beds and bringing the water closer to eye level. A particularly clever device is to build a raised pool outside a low window of the house, so the water can be brought up to sill level and its fascinations seen from both inside and out and enjoyed throughout the year.

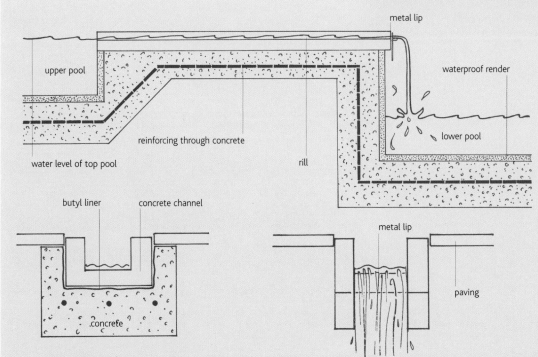

water geometry

There is a wonderful geometry about rills, which lead both eye and water from one part of the yard to another. As with any geometric form, precision is essential for the feature to work well and look handsome.

In effect, a rill is an architectural stream, so it has to have a very gentle fall from one end to another. It will normally be fed from a lower pool, a submersible pump taking water up to the top system – in this case, another pool – which will keep filling and overflowing down the rill. It is essential to have a pump with a valve so the flow can be delicately adjusted. The rill can utilize a concealed pool liner precisely formed to the requisite shape and sandwiched in concrete.

the simple spout

This abstract spout is brought up to date with color, texture, and indigenous planting. The way in which the feature works is almost identical to the urn cascade on page 78, with a submersible pump providing power to draw water from the pool. Pipework is taken through the wall via a sealed joint and then up the back face to turn in a right angle back through the wall, to exit as a simple spout.

The whole feature could be constructed from concrete blockwork, then finished with waterproof render. Reinforcing rods can be cast into the foundation and taken up through the blocks to provide greater strength.

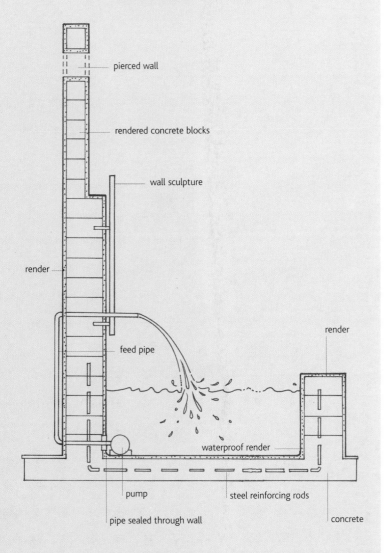

- pierced wall
- rendered concrete blocks
- wall sculpture
- render
- render
- feed pipe
- waterproof render
- pump
- steel reinforcing rods
- pipe sealed through wall
- concrete

above Traditional features can be brought thoroughly up to date; this galvanized tank and spout is cleanly modernist in its conception. It also cleverly fills an awkward recess that could otherwise become dead space.

decorative water

While open water has all the obvious attractions of reflectivity and wildlife and planting, it both takes up a reasonable amount of space and poses a possible threat to young children. Yet water is such a valuable garden feature that it is well worth finding a solution to the problem. Luckily, there is now a whole range of wall-mounted features, which includes classic bowls as well as all kinds of contemporary designs. At last, modern sculptors and designers are realizing the potential of water in the garden and are creating wonderfully innovative pieces. The results may be metal or stone cups that spill water from one to another; walls incorporating slots down which water is allowed to flow; or even, on the grandest scale, a complete "water wall" that is nothing short of spectacular.

Moving away from the walls into the yard, there is huge scope for what I call "pump and sump" features. They all work on the same principle of a tank either set into the ground or into a raised area, at the bottom of which is placed a submersible pump. This is connected, via a pipe, to some kind of bubbling or gushing feature, which could be a drilled boulder, a smooth stainless steel hemisphere, a millstone, or perhaps a fine bowl that is allowed to fill and then overflow, water spilling smoothly down the sides. Such features are usually supported on brick or block piers built up from the bottom of the tank and surrounded by cobblestones or pebbles placed on top of metal mesh. The beauty of all these devices lies in their variety. They come in all shapes and sizes, and they cost relatively little to buy and install. The simplest, which might comprise a bubbling jet of water cascading over stones, is easy enough for nearly anyone to construct, and many such features look particularly handsome surrounded by sculptural foliage.

On a practical level, since the main body of water is out of sight, have a simple dip-stick to check the level. It is amazing how much evaporation occurs on a hot sunny day with water flowing over warm stones. If the sump runs dry, the pump is likely to overheat and fail.

All such features are enormously attractive to children and extremely tactile to boot. Because of the nature of their construction, they are particularly safe, with no open water to present a hazard, so you can enjoy the sight and sound of this wonderful element without worrying about accidents. Bees will come to drink, and those great garden friends, frogs and toads, love the cool habitat, particularly if there is overhanging foliage or a gnarled old log close by. There is a water feature available to suit any yard: I have had water, in one form or another, in all the yards I have owned and never for a moment regretted it.

above It is often the sound of water that is attractive, and a subtle approach is much better than a vast cascade that drowns out conversation completely. There is a pleasing geometry in these similarly sized troughs spilling a gentle fall from one level to another.

right This is an optical illusion, a pair of fun water spectacles that are drilled to allow a cascade to wash over imaginary lenses. On another level it is just a clever feature – interpretation is always in the eye of the beholder.

work and play

A yard has to contain mundane and practical elements as well as beautiful ones. So often these are an afterthought and, as a result, stick out like sore thumbs, when in fact they can often be incorporated to blend with or become part of the overall composition. A small yard is often attached to a small house, putting pressure on the yard to accommodate all kinds of storage and utility items. These things need thinking about early on in the design process. After all, a shed can take a fair slice of your valuable outside room, so the position and look of the thing is important.

Many of us have given up drying clothes in the open air, opting instead for the dryer, but there is no doubt that washing dried outside is fresher and saves energy. There is something sculpturally playful about a line full of washing, and its very presence gives you a feel-good factor. I am asked surprisingly often to incorporate some kind of drying facility, and I invariably opt for those retractable washing lines that are almost completely invisible when not in use. The whirligig type is all very well, but is difficult to get around in a small yard. Although set in a socket for supposed removal, they rarely are and remain an eyesore, particularly in gloomy winter weather.

left I like sheds, but they should be both well organized and if possible engender a little humor. This is a big one — lots of room in there — and the outside is dressed up with all kinds of tools, surrounding a practical potting bench.

above This rather grand affair is called "King Henry's Hunting Lodge," so I am not sure what that says about the owner! However, it is aptly furnished with sofas and lamps, and is the ultimate retreat at the end of the garden.

the garden shed

Most sheds look dreary, sitting with dull immobility at the end of the yard as completely undesirable focal points. Their contents vary, from bikes, garden tools and piles of weekend magazines to a cramped workbench, which is impossible to use with all the stuff piled on top. In visual terms, however, it is the outside of the shed that is important – and that is where a little imagination comes in. First of all, make sure access is easy and straightforward, particularly if bikes, wheelbarrows, or mowers are on the move. Think of the shed's location and choose somewhere that has little potential for anything else. A shed is dead space in terms of garden activity, so a dark, uninspired corner beneath an

overhanging tree may be just the place. One practical piece of advice here is to allow room between the shed and boundary, particularly a fence, for maintenance. This can often be used to store implements such as ladders, which can be removed if necessary. Best of all is to hang the ladder on hooks attached to the side of the shed so it is kept clear of the ground.

A shed, or any garden building, can be screened by a trellis, hedge, or planting, allowing another activity to take place on the near side against an attractive backdrop. A building fronted with a screen might suggest the inclusion of overhead beams that run forward to create dappled shade over a sitting area. This way, the shed also becomes a vehicle that inspires additional features, which in turn become valuable parts of the overall yard.

In the smallest yards, space really is at a premium, and it may be impossible to screen a storage area with planting and other features. If this is the case, turn the problem around and make the shed a positive design element of the yard. Most of these buildings are simple wooden affairs and lend themselves to painting any color you like, which immediately cheers them up. Pick out the barge boards at the end of the roof in a different color, for example, or put on a jazzy door knob and even a stained-glass window. Trellis panels can be put on to the side; instead of boring rectangles, why not cut out a cloud pattern, and paint it white and the shed pale blue? In doing so, you will, in effect, be carrying that great eighteenth-century English art form, the folly, forward into the twenty-first century!

I have seen a delightful little shed set dead center at the end of a tiny town yard, painted up in all its glory and flanked by raised beds, box hedging, and pots. Of course, if you are a carpenter or wish to employ one, you can have any design you want, from the Taj Mahal to Rockefeller Center, but my advice is to keep it relatively simple. On a smaller scale, minisheds or built-in cupboards are a possibility, and in a yard can often be fitted into an awkward corner or recess that would otherwise be dead space.

below No fuss, just sensible practicality here in simple boarding, a water butt, and overhead canopy to keep the rain off your head when going in and out. Neat paving and good planting complete the picture.

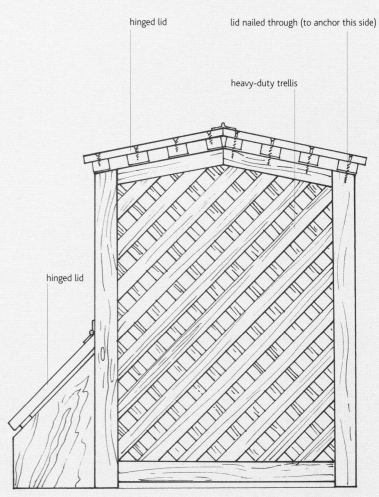

hinged lid

lid nailed through (to anchor this side)

heavy-duty trellis

hinged lid

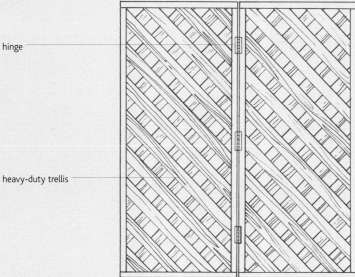

hinge

heavy-duty trellis

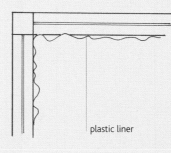

plastic liner

constructive composting

In a tiny yard, it is not always possible to completely conceal a compost heap, so a purpose-built one might as well look as handsome, or at least as neat, as possible. This example is basically a box built out of sturdy lattice panels, pinned into a framework that is dovetailed together for maximum strength. The bin is lined with plastic sheeting to protect the woodwork, although you could use tough black butyl pool liner. The top is hinged so the material can be tipped in from above, and at the bottom there is a neat hatch of ample size, also hinged, so compost can be shoveled out.

right Trellis that is bought from a garden center is so often flimsy, but this purpose-built structure is strong and a feature in its own right. Apart from framing a view to another part of the yard, such a trellis can hide all kinds of unsightly features, becoming a practical and elegant solution.

gardeners' essentials

Compost heaps are often something of a joke, but well-rotted organic material is the best friend your garden can have, adding nutrition, improving soil texture, and generally boosting the tired growing conditions so often found in town. In addition, you will be recycling waste material, which can include kitchen scraps, vegetable peels, fallen leaves, and lawn mowings. Do not compost mowings if you have been using a weedkiller, and do not add perennial weeds, which will stay in the compost and pop up later.

A simple compost heap that can be used in a large yard would not be practical in a small space. These days, you can get all kinds of purpose-built bins that work on the basic principle of adding fresh material at the top and removing compost from the bottom. The whole process takes about a year, and the longer you wait the better and more friable the compost will be.

Such bins are relatively compact and will tuck away into a corner easily enough. They are often green or black, but can be painted if you wish. It is not difficult to build a compost bin from lumber, and it is best situated in a shady part of the yard. A double bin is preferable and allows a longer period of time for compost formation.

Wormeries, in which small worms break down organic matter, are popular nowadays. They look like compost bins but have a tap at the bottom for draining off concentrated liquid manure that is so strong that it needs diluting before use. And do not forget the advantages of a butt that can collect water from the house, shed, or other garden building roofs. Rainwater is pure and will be ideal for watering acid-loving plants if you live in an area with a chalky or alkaline main supply.

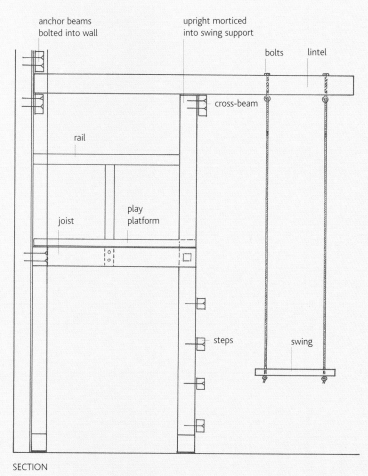

anchor beams
bolted into wall

upright morticed
into swing support

bolts   lintel

cross-beam

rail

joist

play
platform

steps

swing

SECTION

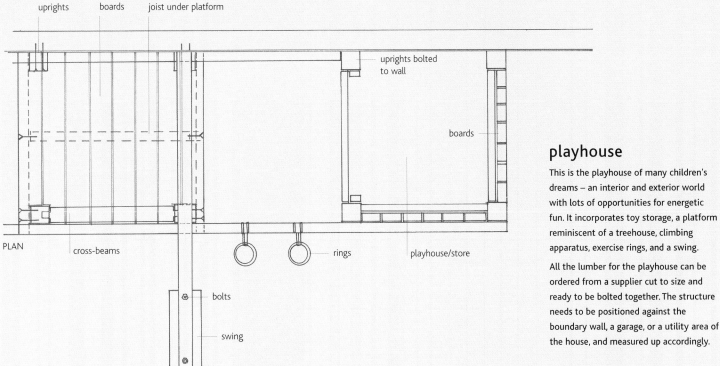

uprights   boards   joist under platform

uprights bolted
to wall

boards

PLAN

cross-beams

rings

playhouse/store

bolts

swing

playhouse

This is the playhouse of many children's dreams – an interior and exterior world with lots of opportunities for energetic fun. It incorporates toy storage, a platform reminiscent of a treehouse, climbing apparatus, exercise rings, and a swing.

All the lumber for the playhouse can be ordered from a supplier cut to size and ready to be bolted together. The structure needs to be positioned against the boundary wall, a garage, or a utility area of the house, and measured up accordingly.

above Children love playhouses and do not seem to mind what they look like. However, it is best to find or make something more in keeping with the grown-up house that dominates the setting here.

for the children

Yards are for everyone, including children, who grow from toddlers to all-consuming large people. Their wishes and needs will change over that time, but they start off with water and sand. A sandpile can be either portable, moved around to catch the sun or shade, or a more permanent fixture. If permanent, it can either be let into a paved area, which allows sand to be swept back in easily, or raised to double as a play surface or jumping-off point. For either, good drainage is essential and is often achieved easily when the feature is raised by about 18 inches above the surrounding surface. The framework can be of planed lumber, which can be painted, or brickwork. The latter is naturally more durable and can become a raised bed or pool later on. In either case, you should incorporate a base layer of crushed stone or rubble 6 inches thick, over which can be laid a porous geotextile membrane. 'Silver' sand is the type to use, not the builder's variety, which produces yellow stains that are almost impossible to wash out. Drainage in a raised sandpile can be easily effected by pipes that run through the walls at the base of the feature. The most important addition is a cover that can be slotted into place when the pit is not in use, to discourage nocturnal visitors.

Some yards are too small for slides or swings, but there can be an opportunity to hang a swing from overhead beams run out from the house. Trampolines or trampettes are not out of the question and are now considered a keep-fit item for today's healthy gardener – although dogs like curling up on top of them and can be almost impossible to remove!

As children get older, ball games become more important, and a paved area with walls becomes a budding sportsperson's paradise. Pots, plants, and ornaments will be pretty much under threat, though, so they may have to take a back seat for a year or two. I was never into basketball, for which you can easily fit a hoop, but I kicked tennis balls at walls for hours on end.

sunken sandpile

Sand is irresistible to children. However, practicality is important, and if the sandpile can be set within a paved area, so much the better. This particular box was constructed from an old washing boiler, drilled at the bottom to allow drainage. Fill the bottom third with crushed stone, clean rubble, or pebbles, and cover with geotextile membrane. Top up with silver sand and make a simple cover, for obvious reasons.

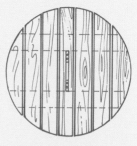

PLAN OF COVER
SHOWING TOP BOARDS
AND BATTENS

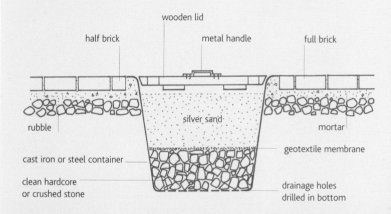

wooden lid
half brick
metal handle
full brick
silver sand
rubble
mortar
cast iron or steel container
geotextile membrane
clean hardcore
or crushed stone
drainage holes
drilled in bottom

arbors and arches

tiny garden, but with imagination many structures can have a dual purpose, which inevitably makes them more interesting.

Over the years, our available living space has decreased in size, so in a small yard a feeling of scale or proportion is important if a feature is not to become overpowering. Nevertheless, there remain many possibilities, from a simple arch emphasizing the tension point between different parts of the garden to beams spanning an awkward passageway at the side of the house. All such features also form ceilings that help to define vertical space and prevent the eye from drifting upward. In urban areas with high oppressive buildings pressing in on every side, this characteristic can be a real bonus, creating a self-contained oasis in the heart of a city.

arbors

There is no doubt that arbors are delightful features, which provide both practical sitting space and positive focal points within even the smallest of gardens. Unlike arches and gazebos, both of which you walk through, arbors are static affairs where you can sit, dream, or doze to your heart's content. As yards can often contain awkward corners or nooks and crannies, these can play host to purpose-built arbors that reflects the style of the garden, whether ancient or modern.

Much of patio gardening is about the creation of intimacy, which means that features like arbors that can be tucked into corners or against walls will both draw the eye and provide sheltered sitting space. While there is a huge range of flimsy arbors at most garden centers, they are often at odds stylistically with your own personal composition. Such structures are not difficult to build; in any case, it is usually the climbing plants that are the stars and not the arbor itself, which can be relatively low key. A simple wood frame with trellis sides and a built-in seat is easy enough, and the components are

Arbors and arches are among the oldest garden features in the world, tracing their history back to ancient Egypt and Mesopotamia. They were both decorative and practical, playing host to grapevines and at the same time providing shade from a relentless sun. Such gardens were largely formal or at least axial in nature, lending themselves to structures that could frame entrances, act as finales to avenues, and turn paths into cool tunnels of flower and foliage. While decorative features are always important, in a modern yard, why not hark back to the culinary roots of these structures? Vines are still a distinct possibility, and you can train fruit trees or the twining tendrils of beans over an arch. Most people reject fruit and vegetables in a

right Sometimes the areas around a house become visually barren, dominated by the building. A useful device is a series of arches running out from the wall, which helps to contain the space and create a feeling of perspective. The area between these arches is enhanced by an old lead sink and waterspout.

left Here is a visual feast of pots, urns, topiary, and fine planting, all framed by the curving pattern of a well-sited arbor. In such a feature you are neither inside nor out – the perfect interface with a perfect patio.

easily available from a lumberyard. Any such structure can then be painted or stained to link with your overall color scheme.

Inspiration for traditional styles of arbor can often be found in established gardens open to the public, so take a camera or sketch pad to make a note of important details. Old books can also be a goldmine, particularly those showing gardens of country houses of the Edwin Lutyens and Gertrude Jekyll era at the start of the twentieth century. You do not need to copy the designs, but rather use them as inspiration. It is well worth investing in wood as a building material – it will produce substantial and long-lasting features.

A trip to any large garden show will provide ample inspiration for contemporary arbors by designers edging ever farther out on their own particular limb. Steel structures covered with metal mesh may sound outrageously avant-garde, but in an equally modern yard will sit quite comfortably, particularly when smothered with climbing plants.

Colorful sails stretched between poles are another variation that is becoming increasingly popular, and the advantage here is that the feature can be moved around the yard relatively easily, as well as being rolled up to virtually nothing for storage in the winter. Poles and plastic sheeting are also rotproof, so there is a good deal of sense in this kind of semipermanent structure – apart from which, you can have real fun with bright colors, perhaps with more than one set of sails.

romance overhead

The garden pictured here is quite the most romantic I know and is owned by a friend who is a genius with plants. This is a place that cannot be hurried through; you need to pause here and there to savor just what is going on.

At the end of the garden there is the most delicious triple arch that leads you into a secret fernery. Such a feature is best constructed from exterior-grade plywood, the pattern cut out with a power jigsaw. One panel can act as a template for the others and they are joined by simple cross-pieces, fixed to the arches with right-angled brackets.

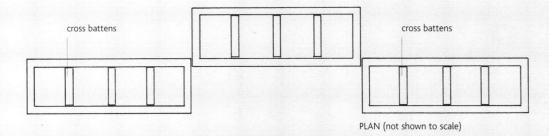

cross battens

cross battens

PLAN (not shown to scale)

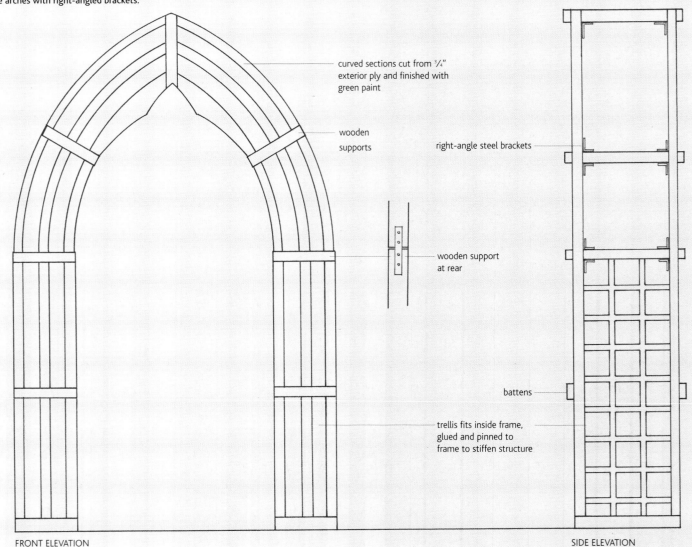

curved sections cut from ¾" exterior ply and finished with green paint

wooden supports

right-angle steel brackets

wooden support at rear

battens

trellis fits inside frame, glued and pinned to frame to stiffen structure

FRONT ELEVATION

SIDE ELEVATION

left This is the view from inside the fernery beyond the arches illustrated opposite, looking back toward the house. It reinforces the important design criterion that a focal point should not only look good from the major view point, but that the reverse view should be just as attractive.

below The classic English arbor here acts as host to a cascade of pink roses. Such dense cover naturally creates a shady area beneath, where a pale statue can stand out in sharp relief.

arches and gazebos

Arches and tunnels seem to encourage you to walk through them. They have the effect of compressing space, while at the same time heightening tension and providing considerable visual drama as you move around. In a yard where you are subdividing space with wings of wall, trellis or planting, an arch will provide the finale, spanning the gap and leading you unconsciously toward it. As a general rule, keep the detailing simple, and remember again that climbers will bring everything alive. Fragrance will be important here; a garden appeals to all the senses, not just to vision, and when you slow down and pause to pass through an arch, there is time to take in the scents. A last addition to an arch is a gate, which will compel you to pause before entering the next room. It is a great device with which to create a positive change of mood or style — say, between an intimate sitting area and a lawn, or from a lawn to a tiny patio. Gates have the added advantage of containing dogs and children, which can definitely be useful at times.

While arches span specific points, tunnels cover a longer distance and are like a number of arches joined together. They are linking features, taking you from one place to another in an atmosphere of tension, mystery, and surprise. The real point is that they must always go somewhere planned and

positive and not, as so often happens, to the shed or compost heap – what an anticlimax! They might provide a way from one yard to another, focus on a seat or statue, or curve gently out of sight, perhaps leading to or terminating at their close cousin, an arbor. Their other great purpose in life is as a vehicle for climbing plants, which often grow a good deal better in the open, away from walls and possible rain shadows caused by the overhanging eaves of the house. Keep your tunnel simple and do not be tempted to hang baskets from the beams; they will just fuss the thing up. Tunnels can often work surprisingly well in small formal gardens, where they can be constructed over or to flank a central axis. There could be a "pause point" on the way, at which a seat faces toward a cross axis that might in turn focus on a pool, sundial, or statue. A sense of privacy could be gained with a tunnel in which the structure breaks a sight line out from a neighbour's window.

The latest fad, fueled by numerous television programs, is to paint arbors and arches with some sort of color. While this may sometimes work in the most contemporary situations, unusual color quickly palls in most gardens and needs regular renewal if it is to look its best. A simple, nontoxic wood stain in a medium brown usually works well, providing a neutral background for your collection of climbing plants. As an alternative, white can be particularly crisp for features in an urban environment, helping reflect light and brighten shady areas.

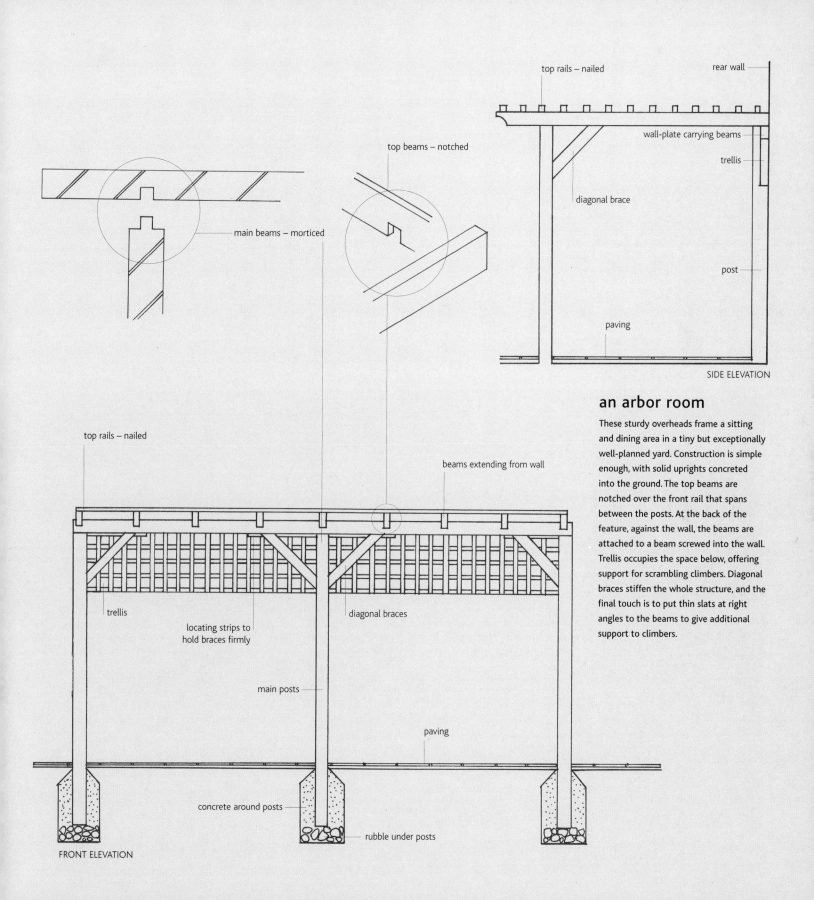

top rails – nailed

rear wall

wall-plate carrying beams

trellis

top beams – notched

diagonal brace

post

main beams – morticed

paving

SIDE ELEVATION

an arbor room

These sturdy overheads frame a sitting and dining area in a tiny but exceptionally well-planned yard. Construction is simple enough, with solid uprights concreted into the ground. The top beams are notched over the front rail that spans between the posts. At the back of the feature, against the wall, the beams are attached to a beam screwed into the wall. Trellis occupies the space below, offering support for scrambling climbers. Diagonal braces stiffen the whole structure, and the final touch is to put thin slats at right angles to the beams to give additional support to climbers.

top rails – nailed

beams extending from wall

trellis

diagonal braces

locating strips to
hold braces firmly

main posts

paving

concrete around posts

rubble under posts

FRONT ELEVATION

ornament

I very rarely choose ornaments for my clients' gardens, not because I am insensitive to what they want, but for the simple fact that this is a personal choice and one that people more often than not like to make themselves. This is not to say that I have not thought of a place for a particular piece or group of pots to go – that is a natural part of the design process and a necessary one – but finding the something that looks just right is down to the customer.

Any ornament, whether it be a classical statue, stone dog, fine terracotta pot, or simply a piece of sun-bleached driftwood brought back from the beach, will have its place in the yard. It follows that the choice is either driven by specifically looking for an ornament to fill an allocated space, or the other way around, where you fall in love with a piece and then find a place where it sits comfortably. Do not get discouraged by those dreadful horticultural snobs who say you should or should not conform to some arbitrary and bigoted style. If you want one of those little men with a rake or fishing rod, it is entirely up to you. Although gnomes are not my natural choice, it is this freedom of ideas that gives many a yard its inherent character, just as it does an interior living space.

Although I have been pretty particular in describing the way in which you choose and use a garden style or

right Such an eclectic collection of plants and ornaments will bring a yard alive in the most personal way. Ornamentation can also be moved around to create a quite different look.

below In an octopus's garden, or thereabouts – this is fun and highly individualistic. Such a collection can be built up over a period of time, and it is always a challenge to find yet another addition to the school.

theme, ornamentation often successfully flouts all such guidelines. A crisply modern piece of sculpture can often look wonderful in a traditional garden, for example, while an ancient pot or statue rich with the patina of age can bring a modern yard alive. In other words, almost anything goes in garden decoration, with the basis that what looks right is right; some things, although fine in themselves, look awful in a particular spot. Your eye as a designer is important here.

The smaller the yard, the more careful you need to be with a real eye-catcher, which will naturally become a major focal point. In most circumstances, one such dominant piece will be enough; it will lead the eye strongly in a particular direction, so should be sited accordingly. However, there is ample scope for a supporting cast of lesser ornaments, each piece of which will highlight its own particular area, bringing it alive in any number of ways.

There is a distinct difference between formality and informality in garden decoration. The former entails regular, balanced pattern, so ornaments tend to be placed symmetrically, either singly at the end of a vista

above There are strong overtones of Surrealism or even Dada in this yard; if Salvador Dali had been a garden designer, this might well have been the direction he would have taken. Surreal it may be, but it is also enormous fun.

right Circles in walls suggest many things and inevitably draw the eye. If they completely pierce the surface, they become portholes to the world beyond, but solid-backed openings can act as hosts to plaques, pictures, ornaments, or waterspouts pouring into pools below.

or as flanking elements. This way, you might have a pair of statues or urns on either side of a doorway or flight of steps or pots placed regularly on each side of a path, with an obelisk or equally fine piece as a centrally positioned point to terminate the view. Informality, or asymmetry, is quite different; here, single items or groups of containers of different sizes balance one another in different parts of the yard. Odd numbers come into their own, three pots of different heights and diameters looking just right in their allocated position.

Simply by being moved around, ornaments of whatever kind have the ability to completely change the look of a yard. This needs to be given a little thought, but you can dramatically change sight lines by repositioning a focal point or even by moving pots around a patio. All kinds of containers are, of course, ideal for annual plants – bulbs in the spring and half-hardy annuals during the summer – that can be changed year by year to bring instant color and interest to the area of the yard in which they are placed.

above This is a dynamic yard, full of ornamentation chosen with a sensitive eye. There is a real point provided by the fine urn here, which is emphasized by the spiral trees and partially open gates.

found objects

I am a bit of a scrounger – not from other people, you understand, but of objects that are discarded or have no apparent value. My yard is full of them, and if I tire of a certain thing, there is no great loss in passing it on or throwing it away. This is not to say the place is a mess – actually it is rather well designed – but to me, "found objects" often tell a better story or stretch the imagination more than those bought at the garden center. They are, by their very nature, unique in design. For example, I have an old iron boiler that is home to a fine hosta; a beautiful and gnarled oak branch that I lugged back from the fields; and a wonderful old grindstone, the frame of which I plant with trailing nasturtiums each year. The grindstone cost me next to nothing, and the others were free. The branch has had several homes in the yard, and each time it moves it brings a sculptural element to its particular location.

Keep your eyes open, think laterally, and you never know what may crop up. A smooth boulder that would look great on the edge of a raised bed; blue bottles that can be set on stakes of differing lengths, complementing plants in a border; or a piece of old machinery that can have ivy creeping over to soften the outline. Beauty is in the eye of the beholder, so find it where you can.

left This arrangement crosses the perceived barriers between art forms; is this gardening sculpture, exterior decoration, or just a simple focal point? It matters little – it has style, a rare commodity in today's makeover world.

right An old milk churn, a funnel of a steam train, or a simple galvanized tube? Again, the derivation is irrelevant, since this highly individualistic container would hold its own in virtually any garden setting.

designing with light

Time was when garden lighting either consisted of one flat floodlight or was extensive enough to be compared with illuminated holiday decorations. Thank goodness things have changed, and exterior lighting is now much more sophisticated and attractive. Lighting essentially falls into two categories – the practical and the decorative. In a small yard, however, the two have to be combined, so an imaginative installation is important if the end result is not to look garish.

The best, and really the only, colors of light that are suitable in an exterior context are white or blue. The others, such as red, orange, or green, turn foliage and most other things a revolting hue. Even worse are those floating, rotating, multicolor displays still available at garden centers that spin with migraine-inducing effect in a garden pool. Rather, simplicity is again the order of the day.

In practical terms, you need to see your way around the yard after dark, so doorways, paths, steps, and sitting areas will need proper illumination. Brightness is a real question here, and a low light value is often far more effective and certainly more attractive than a searchlight. Place fixtures where they work best; lights set into the sides of steps or at a low level alongside a path will be far better than illuminating the top of your head. The

left There is absolutely no reason why lighting should not be both practical and artistic. These neatly recessed fixtures punctuate the face of the wall while illuminating the steps. Hanging lanterns dance their glow over the wider garden.

right Simplicity is important in lighting design, and where a fixture is to be seen, it should be elegant and reflect the overall style of the surrounding composition. There is nothing pretentious about this light – it does the job and does it well.

far right Lights and lighting effects are only limited by your imagination and need not necessarily be permanent installations. It is quite possible to hang these lamps from trees or other overhead structures on a calm evening to produce a scheme of real charm.

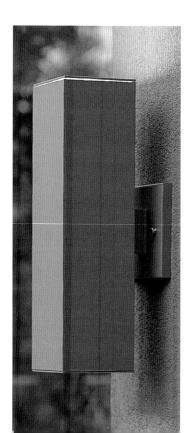

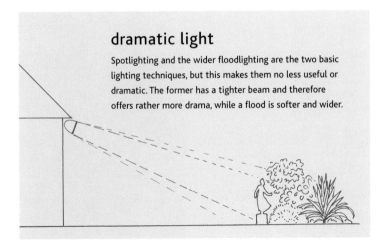

dramatic light

Spotlighting and the wider floodlighting are the two basic lighting techniques, but this makes them no less useful or dramatic. The former has a tighter beam and therefore offers rather more drama, while a flood is softer and wider.

stage light

Buildings, trees, tall plants, statues, and all kinds of features can be effectively lit with grazing light that is set at a low level to highlight all that surface detail. This is theater in the yard, so use the technique wisely.

left Candlelight is one of the most compelling and traditional ways to light a yard, but the flames need protecting from any wind. There is an interesting synergy here between the flickering light and the Arum lily flowers.

right Handsome is as handsome does, and this is a really well-designed fixture that casts its light at a low level just where it is needed.

far right This is another cleverly thought-out variation on the theme. The fins will help dissipate the beam slightly, providing a soft but nevertheless practical glow.

point here is that the quality and position of the light is important, not necessarily the design of the fixture.

At long last, designers are looking at lighting as an art form, taking inspiration from theatrical techniques, which are naturally dramatic. To see how you can get the most out of your yard at night, it is worth looking at how the best of these techniques work. Spotlighting is one of the oldest and most straightforward methods of stage lighting, which involves using a tight light beam, often from a high level, to pick out a single object. In the yard, this might be a statue or a fine plant. Its drama works on the principle that the one piece stands out in sharp relief against a dark background. Floodlighting, on the other hand, has a wider beam, illuminating a correspondingly larger area with a softer light. It is better suited to drawing attention to a group of objects or perhaps picking out a particular section of planting. Backlighting is just what it suggests, using a light tucked close behind an object so that you see the silhouette. The whole point here is to hide the source, so back-lighting can produce real drama.

One of my favorite lighting techniques, particularly in urban yards surrounded by walls, is called "grazing." This involves the use of one or more lights placed on the ground as close as possible to the bottom of the wall

with the beams shining up to illuminate all the texture and surface detail. This same technique works equally well at the base of a tree, where the bark of the trunk looks quite different from the way it does in daylight. We are naturally used to the sun lighting everything from above, so when we use artificial light from below, plants take on a whole new, dynamic character. An ethereal effect is produced when you position a number of low-powered lights high up in the branches of a tree, shining down. The resulting shadows, which pick out the tracery of branches, are cast on the ground below. This is most effective device when used on a lawn or paved area, and a gentle breeze produces a delightful rhythm.

There are also a number of other lighting techniques that are extremely effective in the garden. Pinpoint lights woven on their cables through branches and foliage are charming, for example, while the possibilities for illuminating water features are almost endless. Safety with all outside lighting is paramount in any situation. You can buy low-voltage systems at some garden centers, but remember that electricity is inherently dangerous and if you are in any doubt whatsoever, always enlist the help of a qualified professional.

above A classic uplighter here sends a beam tight against the wall to graze the surface. The pots and topiary balls add punctuation to the line of the deck.

right Eating and generally relaxing outside take on a whole new dimension at night and light installation considerably extends the time during which we can use the outdoors. Simple low-key lamps are perfect, providing illumination rather than drawing attention.

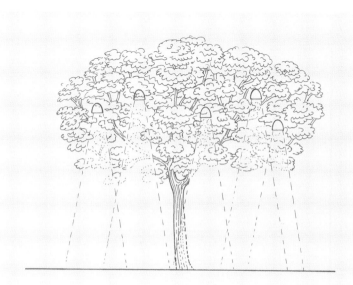

magic light

Light cast from a hidden source onto the ground below is always fascinating, and when it catches the gentle movement of branches rocked by wind, the result can be magical.

blueprints
for planting

plants bring the garden alive, clothing it with an ever-changing pattern of flower and foliage, but they should not be introduced until the design framework is in place. It is this framework that not only gives the composition purpose and stability, but also provides a coordinated background against which plants can be seen as team players rather than a haphazard collection. In fact, planting a garden is not nearly as daunting as many people think. Any real problems more often than not stem from impulse buying and from not paying attention to the eventual size or cultural requirements of particular specimens.

The first and most important basic consideration when planting is the soil. Often, particularly in town gardens, the soil has been worked for many years with little attention paid to feeding or fertility. The simple truth is that the better the soil, the better things grow. Assuming you have topsoil and not completely infertile subsoil, which would need replacing, then the more organic material you can dig in the better. This means compost or well-rotted manure, both of which will add nutrients and improve soil structure, helping to break up heavy clay and give body to light soils. You must also determine the type of soil you have in the garden, whether it is acid or alkaline, as each will determine what kinds of plants will do well. Acid soils support ericaceous plants that include rhododendron, azalea, camellia, and pieris. Alkaline soils allow broom, clematis, buddleia, and carnation to do well. A neutral soil, which is halfway between the two extremes, will grow a wide range of plants. To check what sort of soil you have, buy a simple testing kit.

You then need to pay attention to the quantities and position of sun and shade in your garden. Most plants will enjoy one or the other, and to put them in the wrong place simply means they will not do well. When you prepare a planting plan, you need to take account of where sunny or shady beds can be positioned. As a final point, good planting schemes do not happen by randomly sticking plants in the ground. They are designed with an awareness of relationships of size, cultural requirements, leaf shape, texture, and form – as well, of course, of flower. Many gardeners learn this over years of trial and error, but there are simple ways of eliminating the guesswork.

designing with plants

Many gardening books are too specific about plant species. In fact, it is the way in which particular shapes or groups of plants are put together to look good or serve a chosen purpose that is important, rather than the identity of each. These are the principles of planting design and will apply wherever you are in the world. The different species that thrive in a particular climate can then be chosen to fit the requirements of the planting plan.

A professional garden designer is familiar with a natural sequence of planting that will achieve the desired end result. Designing with plants is not a random process, although once you have mastered the principles you can start exploring all kinds of unusual effects and combinations. There is never any substitute for experience, so when you visit gardens, your camera and notebook are invaluable. Often the success of a garden design is not a matter of how unusual or rare species associate with one another, but of how quite ordinary garden plants can be related in clever ways. If you could learn one hundred plants, even the permutations of how just six of them taken at random could be arranged are almost endless.

planting out the design

This is the finished plan of the enchanting garden that is illustrated in its earlier design stages on pages 26 and 27. The plants say much about the charm and skill of the garden's creator. They are arranged and drifted, selected with guile and a keen sense of counterpoint that leads from one end of the garden and back again in an ever-changing and subtle pattern.

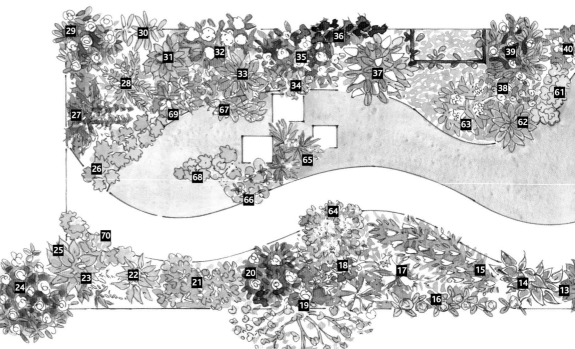

plant list

1 *Hedera colchica* 'Paddy's Pride'
2 *Polygonatum multiflorum* 3 *Asplenium trichomanes* 4 *Lonicera halliana*
5 *Philadelphus* 'Virginal' 6 Mixed ferns
7 *Buxus sempervirens* 'Suffruticosa'
8 *Passiflora caerulea* 9 *Agapanthus* Headbourne Hybrids 10 *Clematis montana*
11 *Hydrangea paniculata* 'Grandiflora'
12 *Aconitum lycoctonum* 13 *Zantedeschia aethiopica* 14 *Hosta* 'Thomas Hogg'
15 *Campanula persicifolia* 'Alba coronata'
16 *Rosa* 'New Dawn' 17 *Lilium regale*
18 *Nicotiana alata* 19 *Prunus* x *subhirtella* 'Accolade' 20 *Camellia japonica*
21 *Aquilegia* McKana Hybrids 22 *Rehmannia angulata* 23 *Digitalis purpurea* 24 *Camellia japonica* 25 *Hosta* 'Royal Standard'
26 *Alchemilla mollis* 27 *Acanthus spinosus*
28 *Osmunda regalis* 29 *Camellia japonica*
30 *Clematis armandii* 31 *Hosta sieboldiana* var. *elegans* 32 *Hydrangea paniculata* 'Grandiflora' 33 *Hosta sieboldiana* var. *elegans* 34 *Aquilegia* Mckana Hybrids
35 *Camellia japonica* 36 *Vitis vinifera*
37 *Hydrangea paniculata* 'Tardiva'

38 *Geranium* x *riversleaianum* 'Russell Prichard' 39 *Camellia japonica*
40 *Anemone hupehensis japonica* 'Bresingham Glow' 41 *Lilium* x 'Enchantment' 42 *Penstemon hartwegii* 'Mother of Pearl' 43 *Lonicera* x *americana*
44 *Astrantia major* 45 *Heuchera micrantha* var. *diversifolia* 'Palace Purple' 46 *Hosta fortunei* 'Aureomarginata' 47 *Buxus sempervirens* 'Suffruticosa' 48 *Rosa* 'New Dawn' 49 Mixed ferns 50 *Viburnum opulus*
51 *Hosta fortunei* 52 *Clematis* 'Perle d'Azur'
53 *Zantedeschia aethiopica* 54 *Viola odorata* 55 *Astrantia major* 56 *Phlox paniculata* 'White Admiral' 57 *Rosmarinus officinalis* 'Miss Jessop's Upright'
58 *Hosta undulata* 59 *Lilium regale*
60 *Thalictrum dipterocarpum*
61 *Alchemilla mollis* 62 *Hosta* 'Frances Williams' 63 *Hydrangea paniculata* 'Grandiflora' 64 *Thalictrum dipterocarpum*
65 *Agapanthus* Headbourne Hybrids
66 *Geranium* 'Ann Folkard' 67 *Pulmonaria saccharata* 68 *Alchemilla mollis*
69 *Aquilegia* McKana Hybrids
70 *Alchemilla mollis*

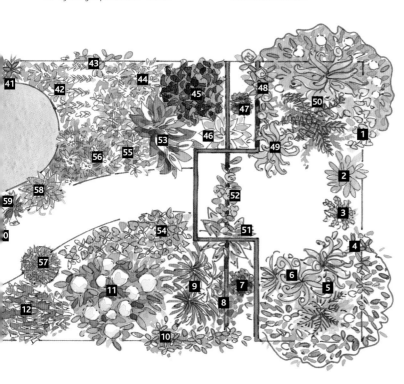

above Lilies for fragrance and campanula echoing their lines on a smaller scale are both set against a cool dark background.

above left The rich textures of the planting and the cleverly controlled color scheme are seen here in full bloom.

right In another part of the garden, hostas add sculptural dignity to a shady bed, where they positively thrive.

layering

Over the years, I, as well as other garden designers, have worked on a principle that I call "layering," which, broadly speaking, is exactly what happens in nature. If you look at a rich woodland habitat, you will see plants growing at different levels, trees being the highest. Below this top canopy you will see a shrubby layer, the species depending on the climate and soil type. At the lowest level of all, there is a sprawling ground cover of smaller plants. In woodlands, all of this will be relatively tangled and untidy, not the best effect for a garden, but the principle of its layers is absolutely right in any situation. It is the reason why natural woodland is virtually maintenance free, a quality that many garden owners desire.

If we take a woodland as our imaginary starting point for the garden plant scheme, the first job is to look at trees, the largest elements of all. So often I visit tiny urban yards that are completely dominated by one or more huge trees. While they may look good from a neighbor's plot half a block away, they are a disaster close up, blocking light, dropping leaves, and draining all available goodness from the soil. The reason they are there is often that their eventual height or size was not considered when they were planted. Lesson one with any plant, whether it is a tree or tiny ground cover, is to check how big it will get. It is not that you should not have a tree at all – it may be absolutely invaluable for blocking a bad view, providing dappled shade, and creating asymmetric balance within the overall garden composition – but its size must fit. In a small yard, look for species that have small foliage, do not get too big, and are relatively "open" in character. When I say look, I

below Part of the bed of the garden illustrated below shows the principle of using a high background "borrowed" from next door. Underneath, the species become lower, dropping down to ground cover at the front. Here we have the transient flowers and swordlike foliage of iris, the evergreen *Euphorbia wulfenii*, dark conifers, and pots of brighter color, including narcissus.

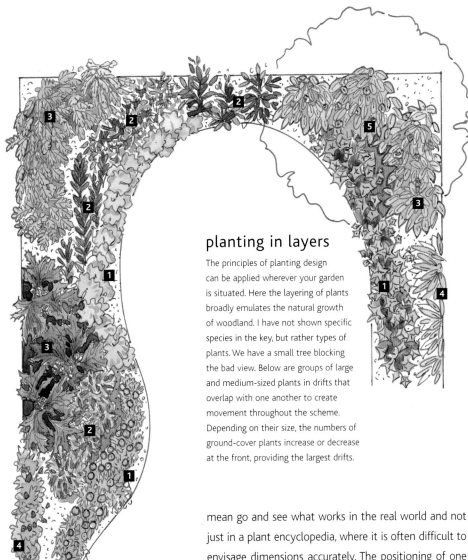

planting in layers

The principles of planting design can be applied wherever your garden is situated. Here the layering of plants broadly emulates the natural growth of woodland. I have not shown specific species in the key, but rather types of plants. We have a small tree blocking the bad view. Below are groups of large and medium-sized plants in drifts that overlap with one another to create movement throughout the scheme. Depending on their size, the numbers of ground-cover plants increase or decrease at the front, providing the largest drifts.

1 low-level, groundcover planting 2 medium-height species 3 tall plants 4 climbing plants against boundary walls 5 tree screening an unattractive view

the spaces together. In a small yard, large background plants may be used individually, while a larger space may accommodate two or three.

An important characteristic of background species is a relatively "loose" habit; upright or strongly architectural outlines that tend to draw the eye and focus attention in a specific area are not suitable. In a small yard, the corners are often a problem; the eye is first drawn toward them and then held there. If the junction of boundaries is softened or completely hidden by billowing flowers and foliage, your eye will drift past with a corresponding feeling of space and movement. An upright, conical species will do just the opposite, drawing attention to itself and the corner in which it is placed.

Large palmate leaves similarly demand attention, and placed against a wall or fence, they tend to draw the surface toward you, making the yard feel smaller. Fine feathery foliage, on the other hand, breaks light up, is easier on the eye, and has the effect of pushing the boundary away. This is why all the larger grasses, bamboos, and plants with delicate foliage are so useful in a yard. It is also a good reason for using small- rather than large-leafed climbers in a confined area.

As your background plants are relatively large, they will probably only be used in specific places, and their exact position can be easily marked on a planting plan. This will allow you gradually to build up a complete map of all the species you use in the garden. The great advantage of a planting plan is that you can determine all your plant relationships and sizes before you go out and buy them. The plan is drawn to scale in just the same way as your main design plan. The mistake that nearly everyone makes to start with is to underestimate the eventual size of plants – both their height and their spread – so do your homework. The easiest way to show a plant on a plan is to draw a circle to scale, representing its adult size. The plan can also be used to illustrate plant color combinations.

mean go and see what works in the real world and not just in a plant encyclopedia, where it is often difficult to envisage dimensions accurately. The positioning of one or more trees is almost invariably driven by design considerations, but also be aware of the proximity of any tree to the house itself or to underground services like drains. Small trees have obvious advantages over large forest species in this respect.

The first layer of planting below the structural trees is made up of the larger, tougher species that provide shelter, screening, and a soft backdrop. Such plants are often evergreen, which will maximize their potential during the winter, and they may also provide an important link with the borrowed landscape outside the perimeters of the garden. For example, you may use a species similar to one in your neighbor's garden, merging

planting in drifts

The next layer of plants will be lower than the background and have greater inherent interest. Here you can use medium-sized shrubs to provide structure, and then you can start to interweave herbaceous or hardy perennial plants to lighten the bed and introduce additional color.

In approaching this layer of planting, start to think about "drifts" of plants instead of using single specimens. A yard full of individuals will quickly become visually busy, with your eye jumping from species to species. Drifts of plants, on the other hand, will give the bed or garden far greater continuity, providing a gentle visual journey from place to place. This principle again corresponds with the woodland analogy. A woodland's tranquility depends upon its drifts of plants, from its trees right down to glorious, restful sheets of bluebells. If you have one large background plant in the corner of a yard, do not place a group of static smaller shrubs slap in front; instead, drift the lower material past the background, leading the eye through and beyond, thus creating movement.

One of the advantages of mixing medium-sized shrubs, up to a height of about 7 feet is that they can act as a support to taller herbaceous plants that might otherwise need staking. Of course, not all the shrubby material will be the same height, and the same applies to the interwoven hardy perennials, which may be tall spires spearing through the shrubs or altogether lower species of a more rounded character. The secret of a good bed is to mix and match, and with experience you will become ever more subtle in your planning.

The lowest level of planting takes in all the ground-covering plants that tend to grow together, forming a carpet. As with shrubs and hardy perennials, there are ground covers suitable for sun, shade, wet or dry conditions. Where your background shrubs might be planted in ones, twos, or threes and your middle layer in threes, fours, or fives, the ground covers can be in greater numbers still. Here you can extend the principle of overlapping drifts, with sweeps of material that link and swirl past the higher background. In many a yard, it will be the ground covers that reduce maintenance to a sensible minimum, but some, although attractive, grow like crazy and may become a pest if they are planted somewhere they are unable to spread.

The general profile of a bed is high at the back and low at the front, with a degree of punctuation in the middle regions. Punctuation needs to be designed with care. Conifers and other upright conical species can become very positive focal points within a bed, but use them judiciously as a point of emphasis. Other punctuation plants include those with spiky upright foliage, such as phormium, yucca, and cordyline, which need similarly thoughtful positioning in a small space.

left There is a subtle interplay here between the solid background of *Eleagnus angustifolia* 'Quicksilver,' the blue spires of *Veronicastrum* 'Fascination,' and *Verbascum chaixii album*. At a lower level, a drift of *Sedum matrona* leads the eye away.

right The spikes of *Veronica petraea* 'Pink Damask' provide vertical emphasis in this part of the garden, while the delightful *Achillea* 'Cerise Queen,' with its flat heads of flowers, acts as a powerful counterpoint.

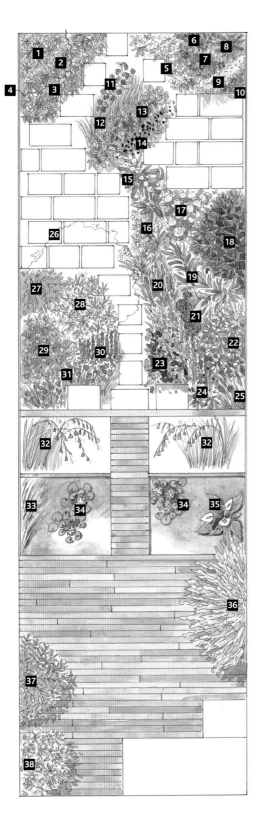

drifts of color

The planting of a garden is what brings it alive and has a real influence on its final character. Blocks of balanced planting suggest formality, larger groups placed in different positions within the scheme reinforce asymmetry, while drifts bring a wonderful feeling of movement. Such schemes are inevitably comfortable, with one sweep of flower and foliage sliding into and over the next with a delicious feeling of continuity. Color theming is important, but so, too, is a keen eye for a subtle interplay of foliage shape and texture. This garden also appears on page 34.

1 *Phlomis italica* **2** *Anthericum liliago*
3 *Geranium pratense* 'Mrs Kendall Clarke'
4 *Arbutus unedo* **5** *Helleborus niger*
6 *.Geranium phaeum* **7** *Rosa mutabilis*
8 Mixed ferns **9** *Camassia Leichtlinii* 'Atrocoerulea' **10** *Aconitum henryi* 'Spark's Variety' **11** *Watsonia* 'Beatricis'
12 *Mascanthus sinensis* 'Gracillimus'
13 *Caphalaria alpina* **14** *Cirsium rivulare* 'Atropurpureum' **15** *Oenethera caespitosa*
16 *Agapanthus campanulatus* 'Albus'
17 *Achillea taygetea* **18** *Corylus maxima purpurea* **19** Veronicastrum **20** *Veronica spicata* **21** *Achillea* 'Paprika' **22** *Eleagnus angustifolium* 'Quicksilver' **23** *Sedum maximum atropurpurea* **24** Verbascum
25 *Stipa calamagrostis* **26** *Cercis siliquastrum* **27** *Buddleia salviifolia*
28 *Euphorbia mellifera* **29** *Colutea media*
30 *Salvia superba* 'Mainacht' **31** *Linaria triornithophora* **32** Dierama
33 *Typha laxmanii* **34** *Nymphaea alba*
35 *Zantedeschia aethiopica* **36** *Genista aetnensis* **37** *Phyllostachys aurea*
38 *Euphorbia mellifera*

shape, texture and color

The shape of a plant in isolation is less significant than the way in which it relates to those around it. The skill of planting design is the relationships between species; consequently, floral arrangers are often excellent plantspeople since they understand the importance of texture, shape and form played off one against another. A variety of plant, leaf, and flower shapes juxtaposed with each other is more effective than an indistinct covering of similar plants, which would be formless. The subtlety of planting design lies in both the layering and the grouping and contrasting of species, the permutations of which are almost endless.

In a large bed, you might consider an upper layer of old fruit trees, underplanted with golden-leafed hazels. In front of this, purple fennel would provide a color break and foliage contrast. To one side, a glaucous-leafed buddleia would look perfect with the fennel and below, in a sweep of late summer flower, a drift of rudbeckia. This combination is in my own garden, but I have used it in the farthest and least formal area of a long yard, where the planting completely detracts from a neighbor's ugly garage beyond.

In another part of the garden and on a smaller scale, I have a fine *Hosta glauca*, with its huge leaves, alongside

classic combinations

Here shapes are used in counterpoint to produce a comfortable composition of classic proportions. Every climate will have its own species that achieve this end. They could consist, as here, of a small conifer combined with *Hebe rakaiensis* and helianthemum.

extending the idea

The same proportional effect can be reproduced in a quite different garden design. Here the rounded form of the hebe is replicated by boulders, and height is achieved with contrasting plants — some with feathery foliage, others spiking dramatically upward.

far left A lowly privet is given elegant shape, clipped into a topiary cube that contrasts well with the foliage of ceanothus and maple behind.

left Pure textural sculpture in the great leaves of *Rheum palmatum* provides the perfect foil for the ribbed foliage of hostas.

right Datura has a heady perfume which reminds us that a garden appeals to all the senses. These pendulous flowers steal center stage, but the plant is highly poisonous, so take care.

above So much of the gardener's art is in the detail – a corner here, a plant group there, an unexpected view at the turn of a path. Nature plays its part – for example, with these self-seeded specimens.

left Vibrant combinations of color, such as veronica and watsonia, are well worth trying. Colors that might look strange together inside the house can look brilliant in nature.

Euphorbia wulfenii, again a complete contrast in foliage shape and size. Woven through is a white herbaceous geranium, and under and around everything the ever-useful *Alchemilla mollis*. This area is in shade, but a similar area in sun might have *Salvia superba*, with deep blue flowers, contrasting with the silver foliage of artemesia. Continuing the drift, there could be the purple leaf of heuchera and then a variegated carex, before the bed is brought to a stop with a dome-shaped hebe. All these are a mixture of shrubs and herbaceous plants, some of which are deciduous and others evergreen, offering variety and long seasons of color and pattern.

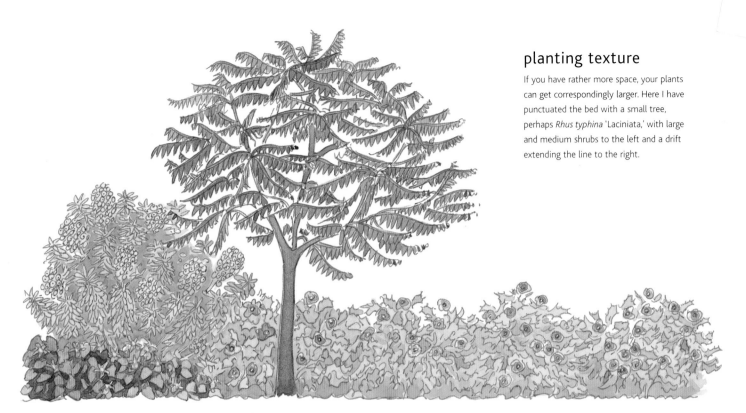

planting texture

If you have rather more space, your plants can get correspondingly larger. Here I have punctuated the bed with a small tree, perhaps *Rhus typhina* 'Laciniata,' with large and medium shrubs to the left and a drift extending the line to the right.

right Grasses are some of the most charming of plants and have become deservedly popular. Many, such as these pennisetums, dance in the wind, bringing a feeling of wide-open space to the garden.

Most designers have their own pet planting combinations that they know will work time and again. Rounded shapes invariably look handsome set against upright spiky or strappy foliage, finished with a sweep of ground cover below. Deeply cut palmate leaves look wonderful in front of the fine foliage of grasses or bamboo, while a combination of finely divided foliage, rounded leaves, and thin upright forms is another winner. There are many thousands of plants with all these characteristics; it is up to you to choose the ones that thrive in your particular location and provide contrast and year-round interest.

left The English cottage garden is a loose, yet carefully thought-out style, which endlessly plays with color. This is a pastel scheme using soft tones of pinks, lavenders, and purples with silver, providing counterpoint and harmony.

color combinations

Flowers are a bonus in a garden, as in most instances they only grace a plant for a few weeks of the year. This does not mean that color is not important, because it does have an enormous impact on the garden as a whole. Although many designers now swear by choosing colors according to their position on the color wheel, the chances are it will only confuse you. I have never really mastered the thing, with all its complexities. The real point about color was effectively worked out by the great English plantswoman Gertrude Jekyll; she simply said that hot colors attract and cool colors recede.

The hot colors – reds, bright pinks, yellows and orange – are the bullies of the spectrum. Place a pot of bright red geraniums at the end of your carefully planned vista and your eye is drawn at warp factor ten straight down to it, missing everything along the way. The use of hot color foreshortens space. Miss Jekyll knew this and advocated that such hues were often better situated close to the house or main viewpoint than at a distance. When you are in the soft, misty light of temperate climates, the hot colors tend to appear even more strident, so be careful with them. In hot, bright places, they get toned down by the all-powerful sun and can be used more freely around the garden.

Cool colors – blues, pale pinks, mauves, and pastels – are altogether different. You can immediately see that they are far less dominant, so it makes sense to use them farther away from a viewpoint to give any scheme a feeling of spaciousness. Grey and cream, in the garden as in many areas of design, are the harmonizers that tie color ranges together and tone down very hot schemes. I love vibrant color, but it can look much better when interlaced with silver to lead you off on a cooler tangent. Another little trick is color reversal. A pastel bed can sometimes become just too bland, in which case I will take a dash of something hot, maybe orange or yellow, and inject it here and there. Not too much, but just enough to give the area a visual boost and bring it alive. Planting design is a bit like cooking or painting: it is all to do with sensitive mixing.

By describing color according to simple and straightforward principles, I hope to take some of the mystery out of a subject that is often presented as complicated. Many of the secrets of planting with color are really common sense and checking out the characteristics of plants before you choose and use them. Of course, experience helps, and you never stop learning or seeing new plant combinations, but that is half the fun of gardening.

planting color

While there are guidelines to using color in the garden, there are no fixed rules. You have only to visit the wildflower fields of South Africa to see how quite startling combinations look perfect set together. The secret is to use groups and drifts of plants and not single specimens that will automatically look busy. The bright orange poppies give this scheme a fillip, but there is also a wealth of interest in the well-conceived background. This garden also appears on page 47 (below left).

1 Existing rhododendron 2 *Dryopteris filix-mas*
3 Existing hydrangea 4 *Digitalis x mertonensis*
5 *Hemerocallis* 'Stella d'Oro' 6 Existing rheum
7 *Aruncus sylvester* 8 *Aconitum fischeri* 'Arendsii'
9 *Allium schoenoprasum* 10 *Mentha x piperita*
11 *Calamagrostis x acutiflora* 'Karl Foerster'
12 *Euonymus fortunei* 'Emerald 'n' Gold' 13 Existing azalea 14 *Aconitum fischeri* 'Arendsii' 15 *Calamagrostis x acutiflora* 'Karl Foerster' 16 *Hedera helix* 'Hibernica'
17 Existing hydrangea 18 *Wisteria floribunda*
19 *Hosta sieboldiana* 'Elegans' 20 *Hedera helix* 'Goldheart' 21 Existing nothofagus tree 22 *Trollius chinensis* 'Golden Queen' 23 *Euphorbia polychroma*
24 *Ligularia dentata* 25 *Thymus serpyllum*
26 *Taxus baccata* 27 *Jasminum nudiflorum*
28 *Macleaya cordata* 29 *Calamagrostis x acutiflora* 'Karl Foerster' 30 *Callicarpa bodinieri* 'Profusion'
31 *Luzula sylvatica* 'Marginata' 32 *Geranium x magnificum* 33 *Luzula sylvatica* 'Marginata'
34 *Kalmia latifolia* 35 *Geranium cinereum* 'Ballerina'
36 *Alchemilla mollis* 37 *Clematis alpina* 38 *Digitalis mertonensis* 39 *Geranium sanguineum* 'Elsbeth'
40 *Geranium sanguineum* 'Elsbeth' 41 Existing rhododendron 42 *Dryopteris filix-mas* 43 *Clematis* 'Perle d'Azur' 44 Existing malus tree 45 *Caryopteris x clandonensis* 'Heavenly Blue' 46 *Bergenia* 'Admiral'
47 *Euonymus alatus* 'Compactus' 48 *Euphorbia myrsinites* 49 *Ajuga reptans* 'Atropurpurea'
50 *Liatris spicata* 'Floristan White' 51 *Anaphalis triplinervis* 'Silberregen' 52 *Thymus serpyllum*
53 *Hemerocallis* 'Stella d'Oro' 54 *Thymus vulgaris*
55 *Thymus serpyllum* 'Coccineus Minor' 56 *Anaphalis yedoensis* 57 *Lavendula angustifolia* 'Hidcote'
58 *Alchemilla mollis* 59 *Crambe cordifolia*

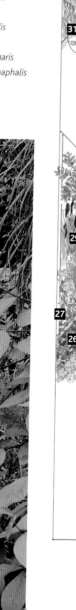

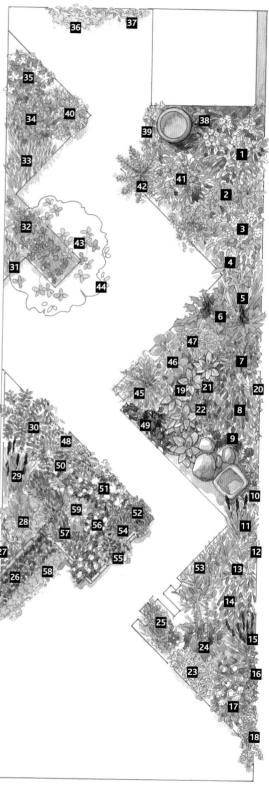

growing walls

To start with, a small yard surrounded by walls or fences may seem a daunting proposition, but we have already seen how we can transform vertical spaces with all kinds of features. To these we can add the myriad permutations of climbing plants, which will bring their own magic of flowers, foliage, and – perhaps best of all – fragrance.

The analogy of a green room works well for a small yard, which can become an oasis in the heart of a city. There is a climbing plant for every situation – sun or shade, damp or dry. Some, such as the broad-leafed ivies, are evergreen and vigorous. Less strong growing but wonderfully fragrant is the evergreen *Clematis armandii*, and the various jasmines are even more strongly perfumed. Some climbers will attach themselves to a wall with tendrils or tiny suckers, while others need support.

Trellis is a useful constructional material, but it needs regular maintenance, something that can be difficult once it is covered with a twining climber. I rarely use it on walls, preferring the better solution of putting up strands of horizontal wire, spaced about 18 inches apart. If the wires pass behind hooks screwed into the wall, it is easy enough to take the wires down, together with the climbers, for any remedial work. The same technique can be used on fences, where hooks can be screwed into posts.

In addition to true climbing plants, there are many shrubs that like to lean against a vertical surface. Typical of these are fremontodendron, ceanothus, and *Jasminum nudiflorum*, or winter jasmine. Often, they bush outwards as well as reaching up, and it is an excellent idea to thin them out continuously, starting when they are still young plants. If you do this each year, it is straightforward, but it becomes a real chore if the pruning is left until the plant has reached adult proportions, when there will be bushy and tangled foliage to grapple with.

Nearly all climbers are best planted directly into the ground rather than a container, which rarely has enough room for a vigorous root run. If your garden is largely laid to paving, remove part of the surface close to the boundary and dig as deep a pit as possible. Fill it with a mix of clean topsoil and compost, and plant the climber about 6 inches away from the wall. By doing this, you will provide a better chance of rain reaching the base of the plant. If necessary, you can pave back over the planting hole, leaving enough room for the stem to develop, although the specimen will need regular watering, particularly when young.

Climbers can be mixed with great effect, but be aware of their flowering seasons and make sure these are various so as to maximize your display across the seasons. Climbing roses and clematis are good wall partners, for example, as are the purple-leafed grapevine, *Vitis vinifera* 'Purpurea,' and the white fragrant flowers of jasmine. Shady walls are often considered a problem, when in fact you have ample choice. In a temperate climate you have ivies, climbing hydrangea, Virginia creeper, and the vicious but spectacular pyracantha, or firethorn, with its wonderful winter berries.

left This is taking climbing plants to the extreme; while this Virginia creeper softens the entire building, virtually engulfing it, there is also a danger of structural damage should it enter the roof space.

right Japan set in London, but beautifully conceived and executed. A stream flows between Japanese maples, rocks, ornaments, and the prolific ground cover helxine. The boundaries have become green walls of shrubs, climbers, and trees.

planting floors

Not everyone wants to pave a small yard or patio in its entirety, and provided the area is not subject to heavy wear, there is no reason why this should happen. It always amazes me how many people think that a lawn is hard work, when space for space it actually involves very little maintenance. True, if you are a real purist and wish to remove every weed or irregularity, the hours can mount up, but personally I am quite happy living with the odd daisy or patch of clover. Grass is a rich, green carpet that acts as a foil to paving, planting, and much else.

Visually, a lawn really will be a carpet, and in a small space its uniform nature can be used as a positive pattern to lead the eye away from dominant boundaries or other unattractive features of the yard. Simple, easily maintained shapes, such as circles or rectangles, usually work best, and if the lawn is contained within a slightly lower "mowing edge" of brick or stone, then clipping the edges is hardly necessary; a snip every six months or so is all that is required.

As with so many other jobs and surfaces in a garden, sound preparation is essential for a lawn. Poor drainage is the one single factor above all else that produces a poor lawn. This can be due either to overcompaction from many years of mowing or incorrect laying in the first place. As a general rule, grass does well in an open position, so dark basement wells are not ideal. If you are starting from scratch, make sure the area is deeply cultivated so water can percolate freely and that the soil is fertile. Sod is the quickest option, and for a small area there is no reason why you should not use the best quality available. If you are a purist, seed is the other option; it comes in different mixes that will produce anything from a croquet green to a hard-wearing pitch for the children.

If you have or inherit an existing lawn and it is in poor condition, you can achieve wonders by scarifying or scratching the surface with a wire lawn rake and spiking it deeply to provide aeration, which will improve the growth. Feeding, too, will improve quality; after all, grass is only a plant like any other. As a final point, do not cut the lawn too short; this simply weakens the grass and allows it to become brown.

There was something of a fad a few years ago for growing camomile lawns. While a good one is both fragrant and attractive, it is not easy to get going or to maintain – weeds always seem to grow more readily than the camomile does! However, there are other alternatives to grass that can be genuinely attractive; I think the best is thyme. As you probably know, this is a low, ground-hugging plant that is deliciously fragrant and often used as a herb. Thyme needs to be grown in an open, sunny spot in free-draining soil. If the ground gets even slightly waterlogged, it will quickly perish. There are many different varieties of thyme, and it can be great to mix these together to get a wonderful patchwork of flower and foliage. Thyme grows well within cracks, joints, or wider gaps between paving that can act as stepping stones across its surface.

Many ground-cover plants can grow and meet up to produce carpets, but most of them are best used in conjunction with and beneath other planting. Ivy is a possible exception; it is ideal in shady places. Many species have variegated foliage and are, of course, evergreen, providing year-round interest. On a larger scale, some of the prostrate junipers provide a dense if slightly boring ground cover, while the prostrate *Ceanothus thyrsiflorus* 'Repens' is another evergreen with delightful powder-blue flowers that will carpet across an area as an imaginative alternative lawn.

left Gardens are naturally seasonal, and first on the scene are bulbs that form a spring carpet, growing here through grass that is interwoven with an old stone path.

right Lawns can be crisply formal or quite the opposite, rougher and dotted with wildflowers. This is the controlled approach, providing a perfect green carpet alongside the stone-edged rill that leads your eye down the yard.

particular places

Any garden has its odd spots – awkward corners, sun-baked borders or gloomy basement wells that seem to defy any kind of decoration, let alone planting. But by now you know that a yard designer thrives on adversity; if there is a problem, it is there to be solved, and the tougher it is the better!

In broad terms, solutions can be split between the purely decorative – where unpromising situations become a positive asset, furnished with features such as pots or statuary – and the use of intelligent planting that will take root in difficult places. While ornamentation is dependent on a personal choice of elements, often reflecting themes inside the house, the planting option is purely horticultural, which many people find genuinely difficult. Yet we now know that the planning of any exterior space is pure common sense. There are plants that grow, indeed positively thrive, in the most dire conditions – hot, cold, wet or dry.

Help and inspiration is all around you, in books packed with sensible facts or garden centres stuffed with plants labelled with cultural information that most of us resolutely refuse to read. Remember that gardens are like people; although they come in different sizes and with diverse characters, they can all make good friends if you know how to handle them.

left Arum lilies are among my most favourite plants – cool, architectural and a wonderful foil for nearly anything around them. I particularly like the contrast of the waxy white blooms against the dark blue seat, which tucks neatly into a recess adjoining the boundary wall.

right If you live in a Mediterranean climate, make the best of it with wonderful citrus fruit and water. This is a delightful little feature, carefully composed with tap, tiles and pot – you can feel the warmth!

container planting

Yards are potty places, ideal for all kinds of containers in all kinds of places. In fact, some yards are so small, or floored with so much hard surfacing, that pots are the only home that plants can have. Floors, walls, balconies, steps and most other areas will benefit from the instant colour and interest a potted plant or group of plants can bring. Pots are also transportable, and therefore the look of a small area can be changed by moving these focal points. You rearrange ornaments in a room to give a fresh look, so why not do the same thing outside?

Style apart, the larger the container the happier plants will be – they will have greater root-room and tend to dry out less quickly than they will in a small pot. One drawback is that big pots can be almost impossible to move once full of soil, but you can fit castors, or choose from a number of purpose-made devices designed to make such things easier.

As with the wider borders, soil quality is all-important; while there is nothing wrong with good topsoil, it is heavy and runs out of nutrients relatively quickly. It is often better to use a specially prepared, multi-purpose compost that is lighter and contains a balanced fertilizer. The addition of a water-retentive gel is another useful aid to stop compost drying out so quickly. Regular feeding of pots throughout the growing season will really pay dividends and I find that a liquid fertilizer is often easiest – but always read the instructions and never overfeed, which will do more harm than good.

The style of the containers will be your own, but a rough guideline is to follow the character of garden you have created. Classical urns do look good in a formal setting, as do containers like Versailles tubs or regularly positioned vases. In a less formal setting, eclecticism can often be the order of the day, and some yards look just wonderful with a random collection that has been built up over a period of time. Sometimes the pot itself is so beautiful that it becomes a feature it its own right and

above Pots can be the making of a yard, particularly if open ground is limited or non-existent. This is a pot lover's paradise, with containers large, small, raised and wall-hung, or simply placed on the ground.

right All those arching, architectural plants like ferns, cycads or palms look great in containers, and as a general rule exotic plants look terrific in equally exotic pots.

left Pots can be large or small, short or tall, but always position them with sensitivity. Boosting a smaller one up onto a stand is a good idea, while standard plants of whatever kind provide vertical emphasis.

left Repetition of pots and plants can set up great rhythms, marching along a wall or alongside an area of planting. These agaves are real eye-catchers, but look good fronting an equally dramatic border.

right Vertical space is important in a yard, so use it wherever you can. While small containers dry out quickly and need regular watering, they certainly enliven this plain background.

to plant it up seems like pure sacrilege. At other times, the container is almost incidental and the planting is the important factor – perhaps an old bucket with a fat hosta bulging over the edges or a simple terracotta pot tumbling with trailing nasturtiums. Humour is allowed; containers fashioned as faces or heads can be great fun with a crop of hairy grass or a cascading fern.

While half-hardy annuals are a popular choice, many shrubs grow particularly well in pots, provided that the containers are large enough and the plants are fed regularly. Vegetables and fruit in containers can be a real bonus in a city garden, while herbs positively thrive in hot, relatively dry conditions. There are a number of specially grafted fruit trees that produce remarkably well and a painted-up dustbin can grow the best new potatoes you have ever tasted.

I am not a huge fan of hanging baskets, but for some people they hold a real fascination, and they can certainly brighten a wall or doorway where there is little other colour. Again, they need to be as big as reasonably possible in order to retain moisture. I find watering the things a chore – but I suspect I am lazy!

specimen plants

Sometimes you can use a specimen as a single feature, providing drama and interest as a glorious focal point within a planting scheme. To do this you obviously need something really special, a plant or shrub that is interesting across the turning of the seasons. If it cannot manage this, then it needs to produce something very special at a particular time. In my own garden I have a rambling rose called 'Goldfinch'. It only flowers once in the season, but it is the most glorious and fragrant plant you can imagine – it is just stupendous. Everyone who sees it wants one and it is one of my favourite species; and I know a few.

On a very different level, many of the Japanese maples or acers can be wonderfully useful. Most of these are slow growing and although deciduous have a beautifully architectural outline during the winter. In addition, they are very happy growing in pots. Such a specimen can have pride of place in many a yard, perhaps in a glazed bowl set right in the middle so the whole composition pivots around it. In one long courtyard, I painted the end wall white, raised the ground in front as a paved plinth and planted a large purple-leafed acer. In summer it looked stunning, but in winter, with the delicate tracery of branches standing out in sharp relief, it was simply breathtaking.

On a slightly less dramatic scale, the specimen planting could be a clump of acanthus at the turn of a path or an upright rosemary bush at the top of steps, ready to release its fragrance when you brush past it. Such plants need choosing and using carefully; they equate to fine ornaments inside the house and are sometimes just as priceless.

left This great fern is simply scrumptious, dominating a shady border with its statuesque proportions. In spring, when they unfurl, ferns are sheer magic and they are far tougher than they look.

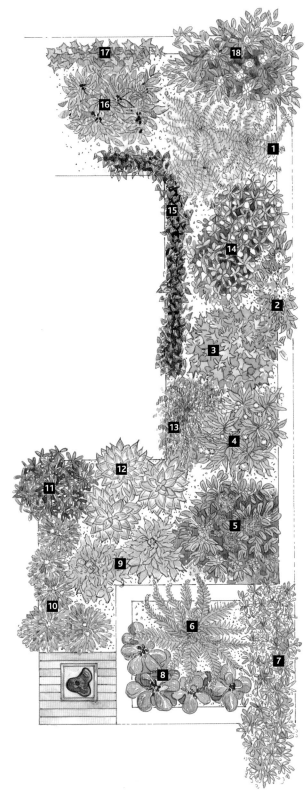

shady walls

I love shady walls, so if you live in a temperate land, here is an attractive and, once established, easily maintained border. Walls provide scope for climbers and the hybrid fatshedera is ideal, as is the gorgeous climbing *Hydrangea petiolaris*. I have chosen a high proportion of evergreens, from the statuesque camellia that softens the corner to the lower-growing bergenia and pachysandra at the front of the borders, while deciduous shrubs and hardy perennials add counterpoint.

1 *Dryopteris affinis* 'Cristata'
2 *Hydrangea petiolaris* (on wall)
3 *Ribes sanguineum* 'King Edward VII'
4 *Fatsia japonica* 5 *Hydrangea macrophylla* 'Nikko Blue' 6 *Dryopteris filix-mas* 7 *Pyracantha* 'Orange Glow' (on wall) 8 *Bergenia* 'Ballawley'
9 *Helleborus corsicus* 10 *Pachysandra terminalis* 11 *Sarcococca humilis*
12 *Hosta fortunei* 'Albopicta'
13 *Dicentra exima* 14 *Skimmia japonica foremanii* 15 *Epimedium* x *rubrum*
16 *Aucuba japonica* 'Crotonifolia'
17 *Fatshedera lizei* (on wall)
18 *Camellia japonica* 'Alba Plena'

above Hosta and Pelargonium 'Fireworks' make good bedfellows here in the shade, offering both flower and foliage for a long period of the year.

tough spots

Nobody said that everything to do with your yard would be easy and there is no doubt that there are certain conditions that are hostile for growing plants. This is a point at which you may need to make a basic decision whether to grow or simply to do something else in hard landscape. Having said that, there are very few places where some sort of plant will not grow, and the right choice more often than not positively thrives.

Many people worry about shade, but I would rather have a shady garden than one in full sun; the scope for shade is enormous. To find out what will thrive in your particular climate you need to do your homework, but in temperate lands the list is vast. Dry shade is rather more problematic, but even then hellebores, sarcococca, ferns, mahonia, certain hydrangeas, pachysandra, privet, symphoricarpos and many euphorbias will thrive. I could go on, but it is best to check out your conditions and soil

again. In my own garden, I genuinely try to do this and I know it is successful when plants start self-seeding all around the place. A self-seeded plant is a happy plant! I will not tolerate anything that struggles or looks feeble; it is not fair on the plant and it does nothing for the garden as a whole.

Any garden needs water, whether it comes from the sky, a hosepipe, watering can or fully automated irrigation system. Yards in particular can create difficult water situations for plants, as high walls and adjoining buildings screen off rainfall or diminish its effect considerably. Young plants in particular need regular rather than vast amounts of water and this can pose something of a maintenance problem, particularly if you go away for any length of time.

I have never had a water butt, which probably shows a lack of environmental awareness, but I love using a hosepipe. For me, there is nothing more relaxing than watering the garden in the evening, and it does not take that long. You get to know what needs water and what does not; well-established plants pretty much look after themselves, particularly if you chose the right ones to go in their allocated positions.

type and then go and look. Other gardeners are a gold mine of friendly information and visiting gardens will give you an unrivalled opportunity to see conditions just like your own.

One of the best treatments for difficult soil conditions is mulching. Mulch can be well-rotted manure or compost, and chipped bark is also popular. I personally do not like the big, unsightly chips, but composted bark mulch, available at garden centres, is excellent. Mulch has the effect of holding moisture in the ground and you need a good thick layer 5 to 7.5 cm (2 to 3 in). It will slowly rot down over a period of time, adding organic material to the soil, so it can be useful to top it up from year to year.

Really hot, sunny places can also be difficult, but for goodness sake do not be subject to that fatal gardener's flaw of the grass being greener! Gardening is about knowing your limitations and understanding your conditions. You just cannot grow soft herbaceous borders on viciously dry banks and, in any event, they would look stupid. Rather, here is the place for Mediterranean or even desert plants if your climate is right. Team them with gravel and boulders and play with sculptural effects to your heart's content. In many parts of the world, this is where the use of indigenous plants comes into its own, a movement that is quite rightly gaining momentum.

The whole secret of a successful garden is to go with the flow, and if you use this approach it will repay you with vigorous and happy growth time and

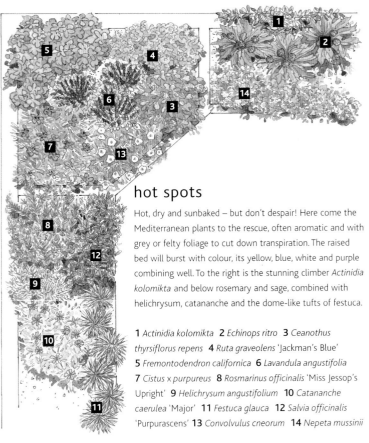

hot spots

Hot, dry and sunbaked – but don't despair! Here come the Mediterranean plants to the rescue, often aromatic and with grey or felty foliage to cut down transpiration. The raised bed will burst with colour, its yellow, blue, white and purple combining well. To the right is the stunning climber *Actinidia kolomikta* and below rosemary and sage, combined with helichrysum, catananche and the dome-like tufts of festuca.

1 *Actinidia kolomikta* 2 *Echinops ritro* 3 *Ceanothus thyrsiflorus repens* 4 *Ruta graveolens* 'Jackman's Blue' 5 *Fremontodendron californica* 6 *Lavandula angustifolia* 7 *Cistus x purpureus* 8 *Rosmarinus officinalis* 'Miss Jessop's Upright' 9 *Helichrysum angustifolium* 10 *Catananche caerulea* 'Major' 11 *Festuca glauca* 12 *Salvia officinalis* 'Purpurascens' 13 *Convolvulus cneorum* 14 *Nepeta mussinii*

Irrigation systems come in all levels of complexity, from snap-together plastic pipe-work that you can easily install yourself to really high-tech stuff that needs to be constructed by a specialist firm. Too much water is detrimental to plant growth, producing a shallow and poorly developed root run. 'Leaky pipe' irrigation arrangements work well enough in areas of planting that need most water. An outside tap is essential in any backyard, and if you are starting from scratch you could install more than one. You can also lay irrigation pipes below the surfaces before you put them down.

At the end of the day, which is always a good time for gardeners, backyards are about practicality. They are creative, joyous places in which to meditate or just have fun. Do not get carried away with all the fancy stuff you see around the place, as most of it is useless. Your garden, your yard, is your own place, so enjoy it in your own particular way!

above left I will only plant species that thrive in a particular situation and all those with thin tapering and tough leaves do well in the dry. However, group them imaginatively; I particularly like the huge musa leaves dominating this tiny yard.

above It may sound obvious, but cacti do well in dry places, and look elegant. There is a design synergy here between their statuesque line and those wonderful walls behind.

right The planting of contrasting shapes and textures, simple and easy going steps and a careful yet comfortable grouping of pots – it is all there!

index

Page numbers in *italics* refer to illustrations

Acanthus 138
    A. spinosus 117
Acer 138
Achillea
    A. 'Cerise Queen' *120*
    A. 'Paprika' 121
    A. taygetea 121
acid soils 114
Aconitum
    A. fischeri 'Arendsii' 127
    A. henryi 'Spark's Variety' 121
A. lycoctonum 117
Actinidia kolomikta 140
Agapanthus
    A. campanulatus 'Albus' 121
    A. Headbourne Hybrids 117
Agave 137
Ajuga reptans 'Atropurpurea' 127
Alchemilla mollis 117, 124, 127
alkaline soils 114
Allium schoenoprasum 127
Anaphalis
    A. triplinervis 'Silberregen' 127
    A. yedoensis 127
Anemone hupehensis japonica
    'Bressingham Glow' 117
Anthericum liliago 121
Aquilegia McKana Hybrids 117
arbors 92, *92,*95, *95,* 97,98, 99
Arbutus unedo 121
arches 45, 92, *92,* 95, 96, 97, 98
Artemesia 124
arum lilies *35, 132, see also*
    Zantedeschia aethiopica
Aruncus sylvester 127
Asplenium trichomanes 117
Astrantia major 117
Astroturf 63
Aucuba japonica 'Crotonifolia' 139
awnings 71

background plants 119
barbecues 71, *72,* 73

beds *118,* 120, 122
benches, slatted 70, *70*
Bergenia
    B. 'Admiral' 127
    B. 'Ballawley' 139
"borrowed" landscape 11, *28,* 33
boundaries *33,* 34-5, 41, *41, 42*
brick paving 58
bridges 74, 75, *75*
Buddleia 122
    B. salviifolia 121
budgets 10
bulbs *131*
Buxus sempervirens 'Suffruticosa' 117

cacti *141*
Calamagrostis x *acutiflora*
    'Karl Foerster' 127
Callicarpa bodinieri 'Profusion' 127
Camassia leichtlinii 'Atrocaerulea' 121
Camellia
    C. japonica 117
        'Alba Plena' 139
camomile lawns 131
Campanula 116
    C. persicifolia 'Alba Coronata' 117
candlelight *109*
Carex 124
Caryopteris x *clandonensis*
    'Heavenly Blue' 127
cascades 50, 78, *78*
Catananche caerulea 'Major' 140
Ceanothus 122, 128
    C. thyrsiflorus repens 130, 140
Cephalaria alpina 121
Cercis siliquastrum 121
Cirsium rivulare 'Atropurpureum' 121
Cistus x *purpureus* 140
citrus *132*
Clematis 128
    C. alpina 127
    C. armandii 117, 128
    C. montana 117
    C. 'Perle d'Azur' 117, 127
climbing plants 128
clotheslines 85
cobblestones 56-7
color combinations 126

Colutea media 121
compost bins 88, *88,* 89
concrete paving slabs 58
conifers 120
container planting 134, *135, 136,*
    137, 138
containers, wall-hung 42
Convolvulus cneorum 140
cool colors 126
Cordyline 120
Corylus maxima purpurea 121
cottage gardens *126*
Crambe cordifolia 127
crazy paving 56

dampproofing 15, 66
Datura 122
decking 36, 51, 57-8, *58, 60,* 63, 74
design 11, 18
design styles 20, 40
    asymmetrical 24, 25, 40, 62
    deconstructivist 29
    formal 18, 22-3, 23, 34
    freeform 26-7, 27, 34, 116
Dicentra exima 139
Dierama 121
Digitalis
    D. purpurea 117
    D. x *mertonensis* 127
dining areas *18,* 46-7, *46, 47,* 71
doors, as visual devices 55
drains 15, 66
drifts, planting in 120-1
dry shade 139-40
Dryopteris
    D. affinis 'Cristata' 139
    D. filix-mas 127, 139

Echinops ritro 140
eclecticism *10, 20, 100*
Eleagnus angustifolia 'Quicksilver'
    120, 121
electricity 15
environmentally sensitive gardening
    15
Epimedium x *rubrum* 139
ericaceous plants 114
Euonymus

E. alatus 'Compactus' 127
    E. fortunei 'Emerald 'n' Gold' 127
Euphorbia
    E. mellifera 121
    E. myrsinites 127
    E. polychroma 127
    E. wulfenii 118, 124

false-perspective trellises 52, *52*
x *Fatshedera lizei* 139
Fatsia japonica 139
fences 12, 41
ferns 117, 121, *135, 138,*
    see also Dryopteris; Osmunda
Festuca glauca 140
firethorn (*Pyracantha*) 128, 139
floodlighting 109
floors 12, 15, 47, 60,
    see also decking; paving
focal points *10, 22, 33,* 35, 38, 40,
    45, 97, 102
foreground interest *37*
found objects 105
fragrance 97, *122,* 128, 138
Fremontodendron 128
    F. californica 140
furniture, outdoor 69, 70, *70,* 71

garden design *see* design styles;
    planting design; planting schemes
gates *38,* 97
Genista aetnensis 121
Geranium
    G. 'Ann Folkard' 117
    G. cinereum 'Ballerina' 127
    G. x *magnificum* 127
    G. phaeum 121
    G. pratense 'Mrs Kendall Clarke' 121
    G. x *riversleaianum* 'Russell
        Prichard' 117
    G. sanguineum 'Elsbeth' 127
glass, garden applications 63
granite bricks 56, *58,* 59
grasses *125*
grazing light 109-10, *110*
groundcover plants 120, 131
hanging baskets 137
hardy perennials 120

heaters, portable exterior 46
Hebe 124
    H. rakaiensis 122
Hedera
    H. colchica 'Paddy's Pride' 117
    H. helix 'Goldheart' 127
    H. helix 'Hibernica' 127
hedges 12
Helianthemum 122
Helichrysum angustifolium 140
Helleborus
    H. corsicus 139
    H. niger 121
Hemerocallis 'Stella d'Oro' 127
herbaceous plants 120
Heuchera 124
    H. micrantha var. diversifolia
        'Palace Purple' 117
Hosta 116, 122, 139
    H. fortunei
        'Albopicta' 139
        'Aureomarginata' 117
    H. 'Frances Williams' 117
    H. glauca 122
    H. 'Royal Standard' 117
    H. sieboldiana elegans 117, 127
    H. 'Thomas Hogg' 117
    H. undulata 117
hot colors 126
hot spots 140
Hydrangea
    H. macrophylla 'Nikko Blue' 139
    H. paniculata
        'Grandiflora' 117
        'Tardiva' 117
    H. petiolaris 139
hydrangea, climbing 128, 139

irrigation systems 15, 141
ivies 128, 131, see also Hedera
Japanese maples 138
Japanese style 21, 128
Jasminum 128
    J. nudiflorum 127, 128
Jekyll, Gertrude 126

Kalmia latifolia 127

landscapers 10-11
lanterns, hanging 106
Lavandula
    L. angustifolia 140
        'Hidcote' 127
lawns 131, 131
layers, planting in 118-19
levels, changing 48-51
Liatris spicata 'Floristan White' 127
lighting 51, 55, 66, 106, 106, 109
    fixtures 106, 109
Ligularia dentata 127
Lilium 8, 117
    L. x 'Enchantment' 117
    L. regale 117
Linaria triornithophora 121
Lonicera
    L. x americana 117
    L. halliana 117
Luzula sylvatica 'Marginata' 127

Macleaya cordata 127
manholes 15
maples 122, 138
Mediterranean plants 140
Mentha x piperita 127
miniature gardens 45
mirrors 55, 55
Miscanthus sinensis 'Gracillimus' 121
moodboards 30, 30
mosaics 58
mulching 140
murals 42, 52, 52
Musa 140

Nepeta mussinii 140
neutral soils 114
Nicotiana alata 117
Nymphaea alba 121

Oenothera caespitosa 121
optical illusions 52, 55, 82
organic material 114, see also
    compost bins
ornamentation 100, 100, 102-3,
    103, 105, 105
Osmunda regalis 117
overhead beams 38, 42, 45, 71, 91

Pachysandra terminalis 139
parasols 46, 71
Passiflora caerulea 117
patterns 20, 57, 58
paving 59, 60, 66
    materials 37-8, 56, 58
    patterns 58
Pelargonium 'Fireworks' 139
Pennisetum 125
Penstemon hartwegii 'Mother of
    Pearl' 117
perspective 52, 57
Philadelphus 'Virginal' 117
Phlomis italica 121
Phlox paniculata 'White Admiral' 117
Phormium 120
Phyllostachys aurea 121
planning 10, 20
planting combinations 122, 124-5,
    124, see also color combinations
planting design 122
    drifts 120-1
    keys to 114
    "layering" 118-19
    principles 116, 119
planting schemes 15, 114, 114, 119
plastics, garden applications 63
playhouses 90, 90, 91
Polygonatum multiflorum 117
pools 23, 24, 57, 74, 76, 76, 78, 79
pots see container planting
privet 122
Prunus x subhirtella 'Accolade' 117
Pulmonaria saccharata 117
pumps, submersible 78, 79, 81, 82
purple fennel 122
Pyracantha 'Orange Glow' 139

railroad ties 58
raised beds 45, 58, 59, 74, 74
raised pools 74, 79
ramps 51
Rehmannia angulata 117
reverse views 35, 37, 52, 97
Rheum palmatum 122
Rhus typhina 'Laciniata' 125
Ribes sanguineum 'King Edward VII' 139
rills 74, 79, 79, 131

roof gardens 60
Rosa
    R. 'Goldfinch' 138
    R. mutabilis 121
    R. 'New Dawn' 117
roses, climbing 128
roses, rambling 138
Rosmarinus 138
R. officinalis 'Miss Jessop's Upright'
    117, 140
Rudbeckia 122
Ruta graveolens 'Jackman's Blue' 140

sails 95
Salvia
    S. officinalis 'Purpurascens' 140
    S. superba 124
        'Mainacht' 121
sandboxes 91, 91
Sarcococca humilis 139
scale drawings 10
seating, built-in 66, 73, see also
    tree seats
Sedum
    S. matrona 120
    S. maximum atropurpurea 121
shade 139-40
shady walls 139
sheds 85, 85, 86-7, 86, 87
shrubs 119, 120, 128
    in containers 137
site surveys 13
sitting areas 69
Skimmia japonica foremanii 139
slate, as paving material 56, 63
slopes 12
    treatment of 48-51
soils 15, 114
space
    dividing 38, 39-40
    linking 37-8
    manipulating 33, 41
    private 45
    vertical 41, 128, 137
specimen planting 138
spotlighting 109
spouts 81, 81
steps 48-9, 48, 49, 50-1, 50, 51

Stipa calamagrostis 121
stone chips 63
styles *see* design styles
sun's path 12
surrealism *102*
surveys *see* site surveys
swings 91

Taxus baccata 127
terraces 45, 48, 50
Thalictrum dipterocarpum 117
Thymus 131
  T. serpyllum 127
    'Coccineus Minor' 127
  T. vulgaris 127
trampettes 91
trampolines 91

tree seats 72, *72*, 74
trees 15, 118-19
trellises *89*, 128
  false-perspective 52, *52*
Trollius chinensis 'Golden Queen' 127
tunnels 97
Typha laxmanii 121

verandas 71
Verbascum 121
  V. chaixii album 120
Veronica 124
  V. petraea 'Pink Damask' *120*
  V. spicata 121
Veronicastrum 121
  V. 'Fascination' *120*
Viburnum opulus 117

views
  framing *21*
  impact of 11, 33-4
Viola odorata 117
Virginia creeper 128, *128*
Vitis
  V. vinifera 117
    'Purpurea' *128*

walls 12, 38, 41-2, 52, *63*
  circles in *102*
  foundations 66
  planting against 128
  retaining 49-50
  shady 139
water butts 89
water features *23, 24*, 66, 76-82, *132*

water, sound of *82*
watering 140-1
Watsonia 124
  W. 'Beatricis' 121
windows, as visual devices 55, *55*
Wisteria floribunda 127
wormeries 89

York stone 56
Yucca 120

Zantedeschia aethiopica 117, 121

Author's acknowledgments

Thanks to all the garden owners and friends who have allowed me to use plans, blueprints or photographs of their backyards: R. David Adams; Michael Balston; Lorenzo Bianco; Jinny Blom; Topher Delaney; Tim Du Val; Sarah Eberle; Samantha France; Simon Fraser; Naila Green; Bunny Guinness; Ursel Gut; Keyes Brothers; Steve Martino; Anne Mollo; Karla Newell; Marc Rios; John Tordoff.

    Thanks, too, to my most professional of editors, Judy, and for the hard work and patience of my art director, Maggie.

Garden design acknowledgments

(l = left; r = right; t = top; b = below)
Designer: John Bailey, London: 1, 33, 58l, 101,104, 105, 135b
Karla Newell, Brighton: 2, 10, 46, 51, 57, 67, 68, 98, 100, 137
Lorenzo Bianco, Cheltenham: 3, 18, 32, 36/37, 44, 94, 102r, 103
Designer: Sarah Eberle for Daimler Chrysler UK at RHS, Hampton Court Palace, 2001: 6/7, 24/25, 48, 60
Bertholdt Vogt, London: 8
Anne Mollo, London: 9, 20, 26/27, 97t, 116/117
Calle Aciete 8, Cordoba, Spain: 11, 102l, 132/133, 135t
Samantha France, Bristol: 12/13, 122l, 128
Designer: Steve Martino, Phoenix, Arizona: 14/15, 38, 62, 76/77, 80
Designer: Richard Hartlage, Seattle for Graeme Hardie, New Jersey: 16/17, 39b, 42/43, 54, 59l, 64/65, 114,123, 125, 136
Designer: Raymond Hudson, Johannesburg, South Africa, for Mr. Bloomberg: 19, 41, 131
John Tordoff, London: 21, 22/23, 35, 115, 129,132
Designer: Topher Delaney, San Francisco: 28/29, 56, 61, 106l, 107
Designer: Jinny Blom, London: 34, 120/121, 124
Designer: Martha Schwartz, Cambridge, Massachusetts for Mr. & Mrs. Davis, El Paso, Texas: 39t
Designers: Eric Ossart & Arnaud Maurieres, France: 47t
Designer: Ursel Gut, Bremen, Germany: 47b, 49, 58r, 59r, 66, 75, 78, 81, 87, 89, 122r, 127, 134

Bobbie Hicks, Sydney, NSW: 50l
Designer: Robert Chittock, Seattle: 50r
Designer: Jim Matsuo, Santa Monica, California: 52
The Manor House, Bledlow, Bucks: 53
Designer: Tom Stuart-Smith for Laurent-Perrier, RHS, Chelsea, 2000: 55
Designer: Tom Stuart-Smith for Laurent-Perrier and *Harpers & Queen,* RHS, Chelsea, 2001: 69
Designer: Naila Green for Spec Savers, RHS, Hampton Court Palace, 2001: 63, 74r, 83
Designer: Mark Rios, Los Angeles: 71
Designer: Bunny Guinness for the Elizabeth Finn Trust, RHS, Chelsea, 1997: 72
Designer: Tim Du Val, New York: 73
Architect: John Douglas, Phoenix, Arizona: 74l
Designer: R. David Adams, Seattle: 79, 106r
Designer: Kerr Smith Howell, Richmond Adult Community College, RHS, Hampton Court Palace, 2001; *photograph by Marcus Harpur*: 82
Cary & Barbara Wolinsky, Norwell, Mass.: 84/85
King Henry's Hunting Lodge, Odiham, Hants: 85
Designer: Jonathan Baillie; *photograph by Marcus Harpur:* 86
Designers: Keyes Brothers, London: 88
Designer: Simon Fraser, London: 90, 91t
Designer: Michael Balston, Patney, Devizes, Wilts: 91b, 95
Designer: Julian Dowle, Newent, Glos: 92
Designer: Bruce Kelly, New York: 93
"Hawthornden," Cape Town: 97b
Designer: Lisette Pleasance, London: 108
Designer: Luciano Giubbilei: 110
Designer: Berry Garden Co., London, for David Pearson: 110/111
Marie & Clifford Harley, London: 112/113
Designer: Gunilla Pickard, Chelmsford, Essex: 118
Designer: Xa Tollemache for *The Evening Standard,* RHS, Chelsea, 1997; *photograph by Marcus Harpur:* 126
Designer: Bob Clark, Oakland Hills, California: 130